P. A. Ingham

Out of a Hop Loft

Seventy-five years of Toc H

JUDITH RICE
and
KENNETH PRIDEAUX-BRUNE

With a Foreword by
Her Majesty Queen Elizabeth
The Queen Mother

Darton, Longman and Todd
London

First published in 1990 by
Darton, Longman and Todd Ltd
89 Lillie Road, London SW6 1UD

British Library Cataloguing in Publication Data
Rice, Judith
Out of a Hop Loft
1. Christian organisations: Toc H, History
I. Title II. Prideaux – Brune, Kenneth
267.13

ISBN 0–232–51895–5

Phototypeset by
Input Typesetting Ltd, London SW19 8DR
Printed and bound in Great Britain by
Courier International Ltd, Tiptree Essex

Contents

Foreword

As Patron I offer my congratulations to Toc H on its Seventy-fifth Anniversary.

Toc H owed its birth to the very special gifts of the Reverend Philip Clayton. Over the years it has attempted to heal the divisions in society, not through grand schemes but in the simplest yet most effective way, by creating friendships between individuals. Many thousands of people have been inspired by Toc H to express their faith by giving practical help to those in need. In today's society the movement is as necessary as it was in the very different world of the 1920s and 1930s.

ELIZABETH R.
Patron

Preface

The authors of this book are of different generations and write out of different experiences of life but Toc H has had a great impact on them both. Kenneth Prideaux-Brune is in his mid fifties and has worked on the full-time staff, in various capacities, for over 30 years. Judith Rice is in her late twenties and has been active as a volunteer for several years. In 1987 she was appointed to the staff as publicity officer and editor of the movement's magazine, *Point 3*.

We are deeply grateful to all those who spoke to us so willingly and so openly. Some appear at length in these pages and the extent of our debt to them is clear. Others are represented only by a few sentences, the rest having ended 'on the cutting room floor'. Yet their contribution to our thinking was equally essential. Our sincere thanks to them all.

We are glad also to record our thanks to Toc H itself, both for giving us the time to write and for the encouragement we have received. We feel privileged at having been entrusted with this task and have learned much from it.

1

Introduction

'One of the peculiarities of Toc H is that it is not a society of fractions of people or abstractions from people, but of whole men.' These words were written in 1927, 12 years after the doors of Talbot House had first opened near the front line in Flanders to provide a rest home for soldiers fighting in the 'war to end all wars'. The house had a remarkable atmosphere and to stay there was to savour home again. Its comfort, though, went deeper than cosiness; it taught the reassurance of diversity. The fellowship and humour transcended barriers of background, personality and rank. At the top of the house, in an 'upper room' which had been used to store hops, a chapel was created for those who needed peace and quiet. Not everybody visited it, but its values informed the rest of the house and a channel of reflection threaded through the banter and debate. The men were equal and, in a war which threatened to deny their very dignity, they were whole.

It was this approach, this flavour – so intangible and difficult to define – which some of the survivors of the slaughter sought to recreate in England after the war was over. They believed that if the atmosphere of Talbot House could be passed on to young men struggling on their own in London, there would be some hope for their future. Their experience was that it was relationships, above all, which changed people. So, rather than founding a peace movement, a pressure group or a society of remembrance, they opened a hostel in the capital city. And from there grew, with remarkable speed, an international movement which involved women as well as men, old as well as young, and which took a variety of forms as it responded to local circumstance and the changing needs of an evolving society. The original Talbot House in Belgium had always been known affectionately by the signallers' nickname for it; and 'Toc H' became the title of the organisation which sprang out of it.

From the beginning, working with others in response to social need was part of the formula. Toc H has many achievements to its credit: it played a key part in starting the blood transfusion service, eye banks and hospital broadcasting and was involved in the early days of leprosy relief work. Today members help in the community in a wide variety of ways, from digging ditches to going on holiday with disabled people to running inner-city play schemes for children, and there is particularly pioneering work with those recovering from mental illness. But Toc H cannot be defined by detailing its activities and achievements. Even in the 1920s there was pressure to describe it by listing 'jobs' or to limit its membership to those of a particular belief. Still more is this the case today, in a pre-packed culture in which the advertising skill of selling a product by tasteful wrapping and a one-line catchphrase has permeated every aspect of our lives.

Toc H cannot conform to this expectation for it is, above all, about enabling people to become whole. Its history can therefore be only a jigsaw of anecdote and experience. The people interviewed for this book have all been significantly affected by Toc H. Some have been involved throughout a lifetime; some for a period of months or years before moving on. But all of them are Toc H 'success stories'. They are people whose lives have been touched by it and who have found a richness within themselves and in others of which they had not dreamed before. That transformation will be with them wherever they go.

The individuals you will meet in these pages are not the bosses or even the clergy of Toc H. A number have worked on the movement's staff; many have not. They were chosen carefully, as people who would present some of the range of character and experience which 'Toc H' means; but in a sense the final selection of subjects was arbitrary. A completely different set of stories could have been told, of equal interest and undiminished relevance.

In 1990, Toc H is 75 years old, and this book is a contribution to the celebrations. It sees the movement in the context of the changing British society of which it has been a part. Lifestyles and attitudes have shifted with dramatic speed since the days when Talbot House opened in Flanders and the people who speak in this book bear witness to that – at times with the sharpness of their own observations; at others by the unconscious texture of their phraseology. In talking to them it has become clear, however, that the experience that they are attempting to express is essentially the same. The form of work, the language of friendship and the savour of their spirituality vary and in the variety lies illumination for those listening to them. But what they share is an unfolding awareness of themselves and of others in all their potential and complexity – a complexity which includes weakness and even unpleasantness. 'It took me a long time to get to that position, simply because I was so frightened', said one of those we interviewed, in an unconscious echo of her predecessor in 1927. 'But I can see now that Toc H has vices as well as virtues, and that it benefits from having people in it who clearly have a bad side as well as a good – people who are whole and entire.'

2

All Rank Abandon

Poperinge is a small, prosperous market town, set in the gentle, fertile landscape of Belgium's hop growing region. Only the memorials and the hundreds of cemeteries, with their long rows of neat, white gravestones, remind the visitor of the horrors that once took place in this peaceful countryside. From the autumn of 1914 until the spring of 1918 two great war machines stuck in the Flanders mud. Trenches ran in an unbroken line from the Belgian coast to Switzerland. In Ieper (better known then by its French name, Ypres) the medieval Cloth Hall, the cathedral and the spacious main square, which were once reduced to jagged piles of rubble, have been rebuilt precisely as they were. It is hard now to imagine the Ypres Salient as it was during those war years, the mud, the noise (and the occasional eerie silences), the desolation of the landscape broken only by the occasional ruins or shattered tree stumps.

Hard, too, to picture Poperinge as it then was, with guns, lorries and men filling the narrow, cobbled streets on their way to and from the front, just a few miles away. One person who was there throughout the war, and who still lives in Poperinge today, is Jeanne Oreel-Battheu. She was five years old when the war began. Most Poperinge children were sent away to France or Switzerland but her father, a photographer who worked with British Intelligence, decided to keep his four children with him. Schools had closed; Jeanne had no schooling until she was nine. Poperinge was nearly 10 miles behind the front line but it was nonetheless within range of the largest guns; and Jeanne's younger sister was wounded. 'The doctor said, she will never walk any more, she will die when she is five. And, you know, when she died her hair was white, like an old lady.' She died in 1917. A few days after the funeral, 'Mama said: "I'd like to visit the grave of my baby." During that short time a bomb had fallen on the cemetery and she couldn't find it.'

Jeanne remembers one of her sisters looking out of the window one morning and seeing a low cloud drifting towards them, and noticing a funny smell. With them was a cousin with her 18-month-old baby. 'He died when he was 27, from the gas.' Later that day 'they came with lorries, and these poor, poor men. They put them down in ditches. And we children, we had to go with milk, and give them milk. Their eyes were coming out. And we sat there and watched them dying. Terrible. When I see children I always say, I've never been a child.'

In the autumn of 1915 the British army decided that one of its chaplains should open a club for the troops in Poperinge; and the chaplain chosen for this job was the Revd Philip Clayton. It would be hard to imagine anyone less military-looking than Philip Clayton. He was short and round (and, therefore, was universally known as 'Tubby'). 'Clothing', wrote a contemporary, 'was always a trial – buttons *would* persist in coming off, breeches *would* gape at the knees, shirt cuffs *would* wear out – but after all an innkeeper of the highest order has no time to dally with such details of artificial civilisation, so my efforts to secure some sort of average tidiness were in vain.'

But the choice of Philip Clayton for this particular assignment was inspired. He made everyone, however shy, feel welcome and at home. He contributed rollicking comic songs, in an immensely powerful, remarkably deep, bass voice, at any impromptu concert. He created around him an extraordinary atmosphere of hilarity. The house, which came to mean so much to so many who knew it in those years, was his creation. That may sound like an exaggeration but when he was away on sick leave for three months there was serious talk of closing the house because it had changed so dramatically.

The club was situated in Gasthuisstraat, in a large, white house whose owner, a dealer in hops, had sought safety in the south of France. The original intention had been to call it something dull and uninspired, like Church House, but a senior officer insisted, despite the protests of Neville Talbot, the senior chaplain, that it be called Talbot House. The name commemorates Gilbert Talbot, Neville's younger brother, who was killed in July 1915. He came to be seen as a symbol of the sacrifice of a 'golden generation' of young men. In the army signallers' code of those days T was Toc and the house, therefore, came to be known to everyone simply as Toc H. It opened on 11 December 1915, just one day before Philip Clayton's thirtieth birthday.

'On pushing through the door,' wrote one visitor, 'I found myself at once in a different world. It was amazing. I felt like Alice when she stepped through the looking-glass. There were soldiers all round me, of course, and army slang in the air, but, in stepping across that threshold, I seemed to have left behind me all the depression and weariness of the street.' There were carpets and curtains, pictures on the walls and flowers in vases. The notices were friendly and humorous, not in the least institutional. There was a garden at the back, with grass and flowers and the sound of birds. There were maps of Britain, not of the Salient, hanging in the hall. It was said that a German spy would have known at once which regiments were serving in this section of the line, by studying the concentrations of muddy fingerprints where men had pointed to their home town.

'All this', wrote John Nicholson, a regular visitor, 'helped you to feel that you were not just a cog in the machine of war but a person with likes and dislikes, a standard of comfort and, oddest of all, a mind.' Upstairs there was a library, and comfortable chairs where you could sit and read. You simply put your cap in the space on the shelf from which you'd taken the book.

Jeanne Oreel-Battheu and her sisters were regular visitors to the house. 'The soldiers were so kind, that's why I'm so pro-British.' One way in which Talbot House tried to remind people of normal life was through parties for the children who remained in Poperinge. The children received parcels, of cheese and sweets and chocolates, and played games. 'There was a big tree. They tied apples to it, and put marmalade or something on it. Then we were blindfolded. The men had a lot of fun with us, because we were all over marmalade.'

Concert parties were held in a big building next door, which before the war had been used for drying hops. 'We would go there. I have still a picture, taken by my father, of a young boy, he was only 17. He was the star, always dressed as a girl. We called him Titch. My sister says she saw him once at a concert in London. Through Toc H she became in touch with him and sent him the pictures.'

Another survivor of those far-off days is the Revd Harold Lovell, who celebrated his hundredth birthday in February 1990. He lives alone in a cottage on Lord Salisbury's estate at Hatfield. Puffing on a much-used pipe, he spoke about his experiences of war and his memories of Talbot House. As a young man he had completed his studies, and been ordained, in Jamaica. In 1917 he was asked to become chaplain to a Jamaican labour corps battalion and he arrived in Belgium that autumn. His battalion was based in Elverdinge and its main duty was carrying shells from the railhead there to the guns in the line. Alongside the camp was 'a large casualty clearing station where I often had to go on duty.'

> It was really an eye-opener. I remember the night of the Passchaendale fight, which of course was a disaster. The wounded kept coming in, you know. Well, there was one young infantry officer who had received a bullet in his backside. He said: 'We went over the top as though we were on parade and then, wallop, I got this bullet. I couldn't move but I did get out, "go on chaps, keep on, keep on".' He was telling me all about it and all at once he said: 'Shove my leg up, padre, it's giving me *hell.*'
>
> I found myself down in Poperinge as often as I could. It wasn't very far away but getting there wasn't so easy because of the shells that kept coming over. But I soon tumbled to the fact that the Germans let off their guns at regular intervals of about two or three minutes, so I would wait for a shell to come over and then set off. In two minutes time I would take shelter somewhere until the next shell went off. That's how I would get to Poperinge.

He remembers 'a milling crowd on the ground floor – there were drinks and eats, that sort of thing. "Tubby" was always knocking about. He was a very jolly chap, you know.' Upstairs there were bedrooms where officers could spend the night on their way to or from leave. But this wasn't an officers' club. Nor was it a club for 'other ranks'. It was, as the signboard outside proudly proclaimed, 'Everyman's Club'. 'There was no rank at Talbot House', says Harold Lovell. 'You never knew whether you were rubbing shoulders with a General or a "Tommy". There was no stickiness about it at all. That was largely due to Tubby's influence over the whole thing.' On the door of Philip Clayton's own room was an adaptation of the line in Dante's poem which told those entering Hell to give up hope: 'All rank abandon ye who enter here.' In that room the rigid hierarchy of the army was forgotten, and the class divisions of civilian society seemed irrelevant. In that room the most unlikely people met each other, the most improbable friendships grew.

At the top of the house, reached by very steep stairs, was the loft where hops had sometimes been stored. This 'upper room' became a chapel. In a garden shed Philip Clayton found a much-used carpenter's bench and this became the altar at which Jesus, who had been a carpenter, was worshipped. There was no compulsion to use the chapel. Yet those who never, or seldom, climbed up to it, knew that the unique atmosphere of Talbot House owed a great deal to that Upper Room. And many thousand did use it. Many found there a reality in religion that they had never experienced before. Many made their first communion there; and many made their last.

One unusual feature of the Upper Room came about by accident. The central section of the floor was pronounced unsafe, and Philip Clayton was instructed that his congregations must be seated at the sides. So it became the custom that men knelt to receive communion facing each other down the length of the chapel. The Sanctuary wasn't remote; it was in the heart of the congregation.

Harold Lovell recalls going to a Confirmation service. 'I shall never forget it because at one point there was a little squad of chaps brought by their padre. They came marching in as though they were on parade, mud and all, straight out of the trenches. I often wonder whether those four chaps ever had a chance to make their first communion, because they went straight back to the trenches.'

In a letter home Philip Clayton described Easter Day 1916 as 'the happiest of my ministry'. He took ten communion services, the first at 5.30 a.m., attended in all by over 400 men. He then went to take services for two groups who couldn't travel in to Poperinge, returning to a packed chapel at Talbot House for Evensong at 6.30. After that he went to visit a friend who had been badly wounded, a journey which meant walking along the railway line and, at one point, crawling under a stationary train which was blocking a narrow bridge. 'When I got back to Talbot House I was more than grateful for my Sunday supper.'

If Talbot House as a whole set out to help people feel that they were not just 'cogs in the machine of war', that was especially true of the chapel. A carpet was scrounged. There were hangings on the wall and pictures and a cross and candlesticks. 'Habituated only to a foreground of filth,' wrote Philip Clayton afterwards, 'to move always among the wreckage of men's lives and hopes, haunted not only by a sense of being yourself doomed to die, but by an agony of mind which cried out at every step against the futile folly of the waste of time and treasure, of skill and of life itself – this is what war meant to a soul sensitive to such impressions. Crudity, especially when muddy, is a tonic that can lose its stimulative value and become merely repulsive. Thus it was that the homely beauty of the chapel, with its inward gift of hope and fellowship, drew many.' One man described it as 'a school of peace'.

Perhaps the impact of that Upper Room is conveyed best by words written on an anonymous scrap of paper placed there in March 1917: 'Will you pray very earnestly for me that I may have strength given me to do that which is right and to make an effort to help others, not so much by what I say but by my whole life. I have wandered away very far, but I want to put things right, and the prayers of Talbot House will mean much to me.'

Talbot House remained open until the spring of 1918, when the German advance brought Poperinge into the war zone. At the end of the war the house was handed back to its owner, and the surviving troops returned to their families and to careers interrupted or postponed by war. But some of those who returned dreamed of re-creating Talbot House, Toc H as they called it, in peacetime.

When Harold Lovell returned to Jamaica he formed a branch of Toc H. 'I roped in a lot of my old army pals.' The branch included 'some quite wealthy businessmen. They simply got on with the job, for instance visiting the children in the slum part of Kingston, sitting on the floor playing games, that sort of thing. I think the best thing we ever did in Jamaica was to establish a school for deaf and dumb boys. Eventually the school was taken over by the diocese and, as far as I know, it is still going strong.'

The spirit of Talbot House lived on in many places, through many people. What was it about the atmosphere of the house which had such a powerful impact on those who knew it during the First World War? It seems that there were two aspects, above all, which people wanted to preserve, and to hand on to future generations.

Firstly, there was the fellowship of Toc H, something deeper than the much-talked-of 'comradeship of the trenches'. People found they could create real friendships with those who, in other circumstances, they would never have met. And they realised that such friendships could transform society. One of them wrote afterwards: 'To conquer hate would be to end the strife of all the ages, but for men to know one another is not difficult, and it is half the battle.'

And then there was the impact of that Upper Room. The chapel was Anglican, but it was not narrowly denominational. The house was Christian, but it offered a welcome to all who entered it. And so those who had known it wanted to preserve a spirit which would overcome the hostility between the different Christian traditions, and would offer a place, within a Christian community, to those who had no clear Christian beliefs.

These two aspects of Talbot House were intimately related. It was the two together which created the special atmosphere. And the atmosphere was an expression of the particular personality of Philip Clayton, the laughter which surrounded him wherever he went, and the sense of peace and of the presence of God which he created in the chapel. Downstairs and in the Upper Room he offered everyone the same warm and spontaneous welcome. He never even thought about their rank or status. He never asked what they believed or whether they belonged to the Church. The welcome and the acceptance came first; such details could wait till later.

Talbot House didn't start with a philosophy; it started with an experience. That experience, and the philosophy (if you want to use so grand a word) which grew out of it, is what has inspired Toc H members, in different parts of the world and in different kinds of society, throughout the movement's history.

3

Beginnings

Philip Clayton dreamed of re-creating Talbot House in London. A large building somewhere near Trafalgar Square would, he thought, be appropriate – Trafalgar Square, after all, was London's equivalent of Poperinge's *Grand Place.* His only visible asset was a large sack full of slips of paper with the names and addresses of people who had taken Communion in the Upper Room of Talbot House. But many of these people shared his dream and although a large building near Trafalgar Square proved unrealistic a small building in Kensington was acquired. Talbot House Mark I opened in 1919.

In part it was a hostel where an extraordinarily varied group of people lived together, each paying what he could afford. Residents ranged from veterans like Major Herbert Shiner, the first warden, and Trevelyan Thompson, Liberal MP for Middlesbrough, who lived there when the Commons was in session, to 18-year-olds coming to London for their first jobs. In part it was a club where those who had known Talbot House, and their friends and acquaintances, were always welcome. And, of course, there was Philip Clayton himself, frantically scribbling replies to the ever-growing pile of letters, booming out a welcome to the throng of visitors and spreading around him the by now familiar atmosphere of chaotically hilarious enthusiasm and dedication.

In Poperinge there had been regular lectures and debates, on planning, housing, public health and social welfare, as men dreamed of the better world that would be theirs when the slaughter ended. Education was an important aspect of Talbot House. 'The standard of general education is so low', wrote Philip Clayton after the war. 'Put the product of the old elementary school side by side with the men from overseas and his mental equipment is pitiful. He is perhaps most conscious of this himself, and a sense of ignorance is far more widespread than a sense of sin.' The pattern of bringing the expert to the group was repeated in Toc H in London, and monthly 'guest nights' became an established part of life there.

The house was always crowded but there was one place where you could find quiet. A room on the first floor was made into a chapel and the furnishings of the Upper Room, including the carpenter's bench which had been transformed into an altar, were installed there.

One house could not contain all who wanted to be part of this new venture. Within a year other houses were opened in London, Manchester (Toc H Mark IV) and Southampton (Toc H Mark V). It became customary to refer to these houses simply as 'marks'. But not everyone was in reach of one of the marks and local groups of Talbot House enthusiasts came together spontaneously. In 1921 the first official local branch of Toc H (in Cheltenhan) was recognised.

The men who came together to form these 'marks' and branches shared a powerful sense that if they had been spared when so many had not it must be for a purpose. They owed it to their friends who had died to create a world in which such things could never occur again. And when they tried to imagine that better world they thought of Talbot House in Poperinge. There the differences between people had been explored and accepted; they had not cut people off from one another. There had been some kind of unifying bond that had been stronger than the divisions. Trying to put that special atmosphere into words made it seem over-solemn (though hilarity was a major component of it); or reduced it to a kind of schoolboy heartiness. But it was a real experience for them and they were convinced that it held the key to the creation of a world without hatred. They saw it as their sacred responsibility to hand on that atmosphere to the next generation. They set out, therefore, to create a youth movement, to bring together young people of different backgrounds and classes before their prejudices had hardened.

Two men who joined Toc H straight from school (and in the same year, 1929) are Frank Field, whose extraordinary later life as an itinerant trouble-shooter in Malaysia and India will have a chapter of its own, and Don Lockhart, now a vice-president of Toc H. To both of them Toc H offered an education in the widest sense. For Frank that included an explicit educational programme run by his branch in Eastbourne. 'Through the winter we had a programme of speakers – one year all the public officials came. And then we'd go and see. And ask lots of silly questions. We learnt a hell of a lot.'

'The thing I learnt most of all,' says Don Lockhart, who joined Berkhamsted branch while still a sixth former at the local public school, 'was getting on with others that I wouldn't normally meet. There was a roadsweeper in the branch and I remember my mother saying, "Surely he doesn't call you Donald, does he?" I remember how upset she was when I started a business and some of the men called me Donald. I took it as a compliment. It all seemed to happen so naturally that one wasn't conscious of it, almost.'

It was to make possible that natural, unselfconscious meeting that Toc H was created. But it doesn't just happen. Bringing people together is not, in itself, enough. In Flanders there was a common task, shared dangers and discomforts. It became apparent that in peacetime, too, some common task would be needed, through which people could get to know one another. Mark I found its first common task in trying to find jobs for the many who had risked their lives for their country and returned home to find themselves unwanted, their dreams of a better world soured by unemployment. One of the first officers appointed by Cheltenham branch, soon to be followed by other units of Toc H, was called the 'jobmaster'. It was his task to assess the abilities of his members and the needs of the neighbourhood and to try to match the two.

In Eastbourne Toc H ran the town's boys' club and it was to help with that that Frank Field was recruited. 'It had run into trouble because they'd got a lot of young hooligans and roughs smashing the place up, and they didn't know what to do. This was a bit of a shock to me because I hadn't met anyone undisciplined before.' But he helped to lead the club for the next 17 years.

Don Lockhart's branch in Berkhamsted used to go hospital visiting, 'which I found a bit difficult, just to go in and chat to the patients who didn't have anyone visiting them'. He felt more at ease on regular visits to a convalescent home for boys from the East End of London. 'We used to walk six miles, take them out for the afternoon, then walk six miles home. The boys were convalescing but they wore us out.'

'I often wonder what my life would have been like if I hadn't met Toc H. I think I'd have just gone for building a better, bigger business, you know, and the real things in life would have passed me by.' But as he looks back over nearly 60 years to those early days in Toc H his main memory is of excitement and vitality. Life had a special flavour. 'I don't think we understood the deeper significance of Toc H then. It was just great fun.'

Later some people, confusing methods with aims, would come to see Toc H primarily as an organisation for promoting voluntary social service. But the first members were clear that their aims were to bring people together and to find ways of bringing religion alive, as it had come alive for them in Talbot House. Social service was a means by which this could be achieved. 'There was no humbug in it', says Don Lockhart. 'It was very practical.'

As the movement spread it was important to codify its aims, to set them down in a brief form which all could read and understand. The result was a document which became known as The Four Points of the Compass*. It was introduced with the remarkably humble, and wise, phrase: 'A further statement of our aims as we begin to see them.' The explanatory wording has been updated on several occasions but the headings have stood the test of time:

Fellowship – To Love Widely.
Service – To Build Bravely.
Fairmindedness – To Think Fairly.
The Kingdom of God – To Witness Humbly.

The response they seek is commitment to action, not assent to a set of beliefs. And they are interlinked. They are not four aims, but one. They are, as a more recent document suggests, an invitation to a journey.

If the rapid and haphazard growth of the new movement was to last it needed some framework of organisation, some

* For the complete text, see Appendix (pp. 131–2).

way of taking corporate decisions. By 1922 there were some 5000 members and 40 recognised branches. It was already too large and too widespread to revolve round the personality of one individual. And so the calm, deliberate judgement of Peter Monie, recently retired from the Indian Civil Service, was harnessed alongside the urgent enthusiasm of Philip Clayton; and a constitution, in the form of a Royal Charter, was adopted.

But both men knew that Toc H must remain a movement of the Spirit as well as becoming an organisation; and so the first Central Council which, in December 1922, adopted the dry, legal language of the Charter, also adopted a resolution which attempted to express, in more high-flown language, the experience on which Toc H is based. This Main Resolution, as it is known, makes clear how central for those at the heart of the new movement the Upper Room of Talbot House had been:

> Remembering with gratitude how God used the Old House to bring home to multitudes of men that behind the ebb and flow of things temporal stand the eternal realities, and to send them forth strengthened to fight at all costs for the setting up of His Kingdom upon Earth . . .*

The Main Resolution should not be confused with The Four Points of the Compass (although it incorporates within it the Compass headings). The Compass pointed to the directions in which new experiences would be sought; the Main Resolution expressed the past experience of a particular group of men. One expresses aims; the other the inspiration behind those aims.

Toc H, its founders believed, needed something else to bind it together. Aims and a constitution were not enough. It needed a symbol and some kind of simple, common ritual if it was to be unified at the level of the emotions. And so Light, one of the most universal of all religious symbols, was adopted, and each branch received a lamp (modelled, it was said, on the lamps used by the earliest Christians in the catacombs of Rome). At every meeting members would gather quietly round the lamp. In the early days that was naturally

* For the complete text, see Appendix (p. 131).

a time for remembering friends left behind in the mud of Flanders. Later it became, more explicitly, a time to be conscious, in a shared silence, of common commitment.

The growth of the new movement was remarkably rapid, both in Britain and in other countries of the Empire, whose troops had fought in the war and had known Talbot House. By 1929, when Frank Field and Don Lockhart joined, there were 17 marks and just over 400 branches and groups in Britain, with a further 200 branches and groups overseas. By 1938 the number of marks had risen to 21. There were over 1000 branches and groups in Britain and nearly 400 overseas. And a parallel movement for women had grown equally rapidly.

4

'Ballad of the Slums'

'I don't remember people talking about getting married when I was at school. I think most of us rather looked down on people who were interested in boys or wanted to get married. Strange how attitudes change, isn't it? I think now girls would probably rather look down on others who didn't get a boy-friend. We did the opposite. If someone wanted to go around with boys, well, she wasn't worth knowing, was she?'

Constance Beazley was born in a Surrey village in 1917. All her teachers were unmarried: some had lost fiancés in the First World War; some had chosen a career instead – for if they did marry, they were obliged to give up working. She suspects that generally they regarded marriage as beneath them. But they also had strict ideas about what constituted a suitable career for a Grammar School product: 'They had the attitude that you must follow an academic career or you must do something that required you to use your brain, otherwise your brains were wasted. There were not so many occupations open to girls in those days that were generally known about. There was the Civil Service or teaching . . . and nursing was something you could go and do if you didn't have any brains.' When they discovered that they could not shift Constance's determination to be a nurse they 'washed their hands of me . . . *that* was just domestic work and why educate people if all they're going to do is go and scrub floors?'

But Constance had a rather different vision: 'I loved children. I'd read lots of Victorian books about little children in the slums of London. I wanted to go and work in the East End of London which was just something in my imagination, and I wanted to look after children.' All the young women with whom she did her three year training were middle class, with the exception of a few from wealthier backgrounds. Most of them had gone to Grammar School – a few to boarding schools: 'They were more particular about that than about educational qualifications.' The East End was very different from the world they were used to: 'There were children who were in hospital simply because they didn't have enough to eat, because there wasn't enough money and they came from overcrowded families.' There was little birth control and a high infant mortality rate – the student nurses had to get used to becoming attached to babies only to see them die.

They had very little free time. There were a few lectures and exams but the course was 'really an apprenticeship'. They had to live in the nurses' home, could not go out after coming off duty and had to be in bed by 10 p.m. But after the Sister had been round to check that all the lights were out, the girls would gather in one of the rooms and put the world to rights. These all-female discussions were an attempt to wrestle with their experiences and the contrast with their comfortable upbringings. There was little political awareness and they were certainly 'not militant'. Rather, they talked 'just about life in general, about what was good and what was bad; what was important and what wasn't. Social problems . . . yes, quite a bit. We wanted things put right but it never occurred to us that we could do anything about it.'

With very little access to radios or newspapers, they were cut off from the outside world. They were also very hard up. They occasionally received free tickets for the theatre, for plays that were a flop – evening dress was obligatory and since they only had one or two between them they would share them around. Nevertheless, they had 'a whale of a time'. Constance enjoyed her own company and spent many hours wandering around the Embankment, Blackfriars and Fleet Street – all areas which were within walking distance, and with which she fell in love. She could afford to spend 6d on her one day off and this would pay for a cup of tea and a bun, or a ride on top of a bus, or a Penguin paperback. She usually chose the latter, and took it to a park to read.

In those years she also made frequent visits to All Hallows, the Guild Church of Toc H situated next to the Tower of London. She had 'fallen for Toc H' at the age of 15, after being captivated by a poem in the *Toc H Journal* which her brother, who was involved while at college, lent her. Almost 60 years later, she can still remember the lines:

> Open my eyes to visions girt with wonder
> And with beauty lit
> But ever let me see the dirt
> And all that spawn and die in it.
> Open my ears to music;
> Let me thrill to spring's first flutes and drums
> But never let me dare forget
> The bitter ballad of the slums.

They would probably cause a modern 15-year-old to smile or wince, but they 'absolutely fitted what I was feeling at that time. They linked my childhood background, which was all fields and trees and rivers and lovely things with this burning desire I had to go and live in the slums . . . I had a feeling that I ought not to be enjoying these lovely things because those other things existed.'

It was a feeling she shared with many contemporaries, brought up in a land intended to be 'fit for heroes to live in'; for which fathers, uncles and brothers had died. When she read the original Toc H literature, describing events in Talbot House, it seemed totally relevant. The war had been such a part of her childhood that she had taken it for granted. On Armistice Day, at school, 'lots of the teachers used to cry – you just accepted it'. She had the postcards her father had sent her from the Front (although 'he never spoke of it') and her older brother and sister had certificates for collecting eggs for wounded soldiers. And they were the fortunate ones; she remembers contemporaries whose fathers had died or who had a bad chest or some other ailment 'because of the war'. There was an inbuilt sense of service of a self-denying sort. The women of her generation, although their memories are all of laughter and companionship, describe the Toc H ideal as one of sacrifice.

Although the Toc H women gradually took on similar tasks and patterns of organisation to the men, their role was initially more narrowly defined and summarised in the name of their organisation, 'The League of Women Helpers'. They were to *support* the men and free them from mundane tasks: their role in the 'Toc H family' was to be much the same as the traditional one of wives, mothers and sisters. The original members were nurses who had been serving with the Red Cross in Belgium and had gone to Talbot House in search of an English church service at Easter. One of them, Alison Macfie, became a great friend of Tubby Clayton and was drawn into the postwar fervour of finding ways of 'maintaining the old fellowship and extending it to the younger clerks, civil servants and students of London'. One of their very first tasks was the sewing of curtains for one of the early hostels, and: 'The three Ms – mending, making and money-raising – indeed formed an important part of our early basic contribution', wrote 'Mac', as she became known. But she also recounts early attempts to convert her fellow members 'to the view that LWH should eventually rise to be less of a handmaid and more of a partner to Toc H'. It was to take many years for this to become the prevailing view – the organisation changed its name to 'The Women's Association' in 1952 and did not integrate with Toc H itself until 1971.

Yet for many the League offered a *liberation* from conventional constraints, and this was certainly a part of its ideal. The original design for an LWH stained glass window of St Clare, intended for the crypt at All Hallows, showed her with a halo over her head and a lily in her hand. When Clayton saw it he made an emphatic complaint. St Clare had not been like that at all, he protested: she was a 'bobbed-haired, cigarette-smoking society girl who's got religion badly'. And this is how the final window depicted her.

It was an image as romantic as the original. An enormous range of women did become involved, but the most active and prominent were blue-stockinged rather than sequinned. Jennifer Mitchell, who joined The Women's Association staff at the age of 22 in the mid 1960s, was deeply impressed by the calibre of her older colleagues. They were the sort who went to be missionaries: 'They were incredibly sane, incredibly dedicated, religious if you like – they were a breed of women head and shoulders above many others in this country.' They spent many years travelling around the country on their own forming 'amazingly good relationships' with members. They took little for granted – money was short (they didn't have the benefit of the donations and inheritances lavished on the men's organisation) and they felt they had to account for every penny spent. Both time and fellowship were precious. They were a tight-knit little community – the staff consisted of only about 12 people in her day as opposed to the 70 or 80 on the men's side. In the earlier days, staff conferences were held in individual's houses. And for most of them, Toc H was their life. The women who worked for Toc H rarely married, for careers and families were still alternatives.

One exception to this rule was Elisabeth Worth, who was employed by Toc H for many years before and after the Second World War. In 1940 she married an Anglican priest whom she met through Toc H. She felt unable to travel or to stay away from home as much as some of her colleagues because of her domestic and family responsibilities – and she knows that she 'missed out on a lot of the fun' as a result.

She was also slightly unusual in her background – almost a 'society girl' in fact. Her father was a successful barrister and Elisabeth went to Cheltenham Ladies' College. She was on the point of going on to London University when her father became a Judge, moved to Suffolk and summoned her to be his hostess since he had been divorced for many years. 'That was the way parents behaved in those days. He trained me up very well!' Three years later he remarried and she was free to return to the capital; but it was too late to take up her degree course and she trained as a secretary instead. 'By great good fortune' she met Toc H at this time and was quickly on the staff. She was painfully shy and used to a household of men, so that she found the all-female environment difficult. But she soon found great warmth among these people and the work was stimulating. She discovered that she liked to solve problems and there were plenty for her to tackle here – especially in later years when she was, for a long time, International Secretary. She had acquired a career; but also, and more important, she had found the 'cause' she had unknowingly been looking for.

Constance Beazley had had little incentive to follow up her original, teenage, attraction to the movement. Her career flourished – after the war she went on to further training and became a nursing tutor – and fulfilled both her intellectual and 'caring' needs. She collected a series of LWH booklets, but had only one actual encounter with its members; one which had few echoes of the 'bitter ballad of the slums'. During the 'phoney war' (1938–9) she was working in Bexhill-on-Sea and went along to the Toc H branch there. She recalls arriving on her bike in her navy blue raincoat, to be ushered into a drawing room where half a dozen ladies wearing hats were sitting around a silver teapot. She can remember no activities other than a visit to a baker's for a demonstration of how to ice a cake, and a talk from one of the members about her holiday. The remarkable thing was that she was not in the least bit disillusioned.

Several years later she remembered Toc H and became involved in a rather more lively branch. She has no idea why she thought of it again. It was a time when she was afflicted with a profound sense of futility. The war had sucked her dry of idealism. 'I had this sort of attitude – well, what does it matter anyway 'cause the world'll probably end tomorrow and if it doesn't it'll go on as it does now. I felt like they did after the First War – "this is the way the world ends, not with a bang but a whimper".'

Through Toc H, she rediscovered a sense of purpose and direction: 'The exhilaration of striving with others for a common cause, a better world.' But it was not so much that it gave her tasks to do, as that it effected a transformation *within* her. She had never been a sociable person and there had only ever been a few individuals with whom she wanted to spend a lot of time. As for the rest, as long as she didn't harm anyone, she felt that nothing more was required. Now, she realised that even when she didn't feel like mixing, other people might need *her* – more than that, 'in Toc H I sort of loved everybody!' It was refreshing to spend time with people who had nothing to do with her profession – shop and office workers, housewives, a woman who worked in the city and another who ran a canteen. A part of her that had felt empty and useless came alive: 'Toc H altered my attitude to people. Because although superficially I was nice to people I didn't really care a hang about them – except the ones I was looking after. It made me realise that life was pretty hollow unless you had something worthwhile, a purpose in life, a social conscience . . .'

Many of the people she came to know had a strong religious faith. There were one or two who impressed her powerfully by their simple, practical living out of the Gospels – unassuming and unspectacular characters, women who had led obscure and loving lives, often in great adversity. Her interest was also aroused by the prayers and services which featured so strongly in Toc H life. She had no religious belief of her own although she knew the Bible 'inside out and backwards' from her childhood. Her parents were Strict and Particular Baptists, whose lives were governed by their faith. It made them committed and kindly members of the community, but disapproving of a number of pastimes. When Constance went to the cinema with a group of fellow-students, it was her first visit. She concealed the fact – clinging close to the others in some anxiety when the lights went out and the floor started to slope up! She had paid little attention when taken to church as a little girl, preferring to entertain herself by examining the ladies' hats. But her curiosity was aroused by her Toc H encounters. She borrowed a *Book of Common Prayer* from one member, and then other books from members of different denominations. She looked into religious history and went round all the different Churches as an experiment, until she settled on the Presbyterians, where she has remained.

But the real 'conversion experience' of Constance's life was that effected by Toc H itself – slowly, without her realising what was going on. This is what she values about the movement above all: 'The important thing about Toc H is what it does to you. Because doing something *to* you it will do something *through* you. I do feel this very strongly. I suppose this is why it didn't matter to me when there wasn't a branch to go to – it didn't make a ha'porth of difference. Anything that's worthwhile that I do, is largely the result of Toc H in me.'

5

A Touch of Home

The Services' Club run by Toc H in Plymouth was the only one in the city to escape the bombs. Its single small electric cooking square was soon over-used as long queues of sailors came in search of food and company. Alice Welford, who was then a young member of staff working for The League of Women Helpers in the West Country, remembers these as very happy days despite the trauma and tragedy of the war: 'It was a marvellous time – it was a wonderful time. It was such fun! I wouldn't have missed it for the world.'

Everybody was keen to help. The cook turned up every day without fail and one man from the country brought in a supply of eggs every single morning. Alice, now aged over 80 – a tiny lady of enormous charm and warmth – laughingly recalls an occasion when she was reluctant to supply one particular Petty Officer with one of these eggs. He was 'rather tiddly' and had also asked for a glass of milk – Alice was convinced that he was going to throw them at her. Her personal experience had not acquainted her with this cocktail as a cure for a hangover.

The delicate, genteel modulations of Alice's voice give a clue to her sheltered, 'beautiful childhood' in a Cheshire village. Her father was a solicitor in Manchester but she and her brothers and sister were only taken up to the city once a year for the Christmas pantomime. Her circle was limited and she had no contact with the worlds of industry and commerce. Only when she joined Stockport women's branch of Toc H did she find herself suddenly mixing with girls who worked in factories or served behind counters, as well as with women who did not need to go out to work or those, like herself, in the teaching profession. It could have been a great strain but she remembers above all the warmth and friendliness and the sense that here she could say whatever she liked.

In fact it was 'service' – the opportunity to help those less fortunate than herself – which had originally attracted her to Toc H, rather than the variety of people it offered to introduce her to. But the two were inextricably linked. She was not given her own 'job' to do until she had learned what 'service' really meant. She remembers being told that she was 'to go with Norah' the following week to take books round the workhouse hospital:

> And I was horrified and I daren't say 'no' because I knew why I had joined Toc H. I didn't go to sleep properly the night before and I certainly did not want to go into a workhouse hospital . . . I remember turning up on the tram and getting off outside this grim building and being met by Norah . . . now this is another part of Toc H training. I didn't *know* Norah. I knew her as Norah who sat over there in the meetings, but we didn't have any kind of close relationship . . . Anyway, as we walked across from these big main gates to the door of the hospital she said: 'Now we haven't come here just to give out books. Books are a means to an end. We've come here to get to know these poor souls in the beds.' And I thought, 'I'm not going to like this. I'm sure I'm going to see somebody without any legs. I don't know what I shall do.' We went through the swing doors of this rather grim hospital and there, coming down the long corridor in a wheelchair was a little old lady and she had no legs. There was this little torso sitting there. And instantly I realised that I didn't mind. I was just terribly, terribly sorry for her. And that was the start of a month's taking books round the hospital. I couldn't *wait* for the next week. So I owe Toc H a great deal, you see, right from the start . . . And I got to know Norah because I went with her for a month and they had known in the branch that I didn't know Norah . . .

There were good relationships with the men. The women helped them with the canteen they used to run in the Stockport slums and she has memories of taking girls from these same slums for a weekend in the Pennines where the men were running a project. The girls 'all slept together in a large barn, peeling potatoes outside on a cold morning; and the men came along and helped us and it was all so natural . . . we didn't have any kind of a division with the men.' The first big festival she attended, in Liverpool, was also mixed. But here the real excitement was the gathering together of people from all over the country:

> We slept on the floor on mattresses in a girls' gymnasium. At least I say we slept – I don't think we did! I wondered what on earth I'd come to because it was so noisy with people singing and not going to sleep at all. It really was very trying and I thought 'This is mad!' And then we washed in cold water in the early morning and went off to our respective churches for Holy Communion. And then we went to a cafe for breakfast and it wasn't open yet so we sat on the pavement . . . they were very jolly days. And Tubby came to speak to us later in the afternoon with his shirtsleeves rolled up, standing on the top of the table in the gymnasium and we were sitting on the floor and it was a very very happy weekend.

But if relations between the men and women were good in the 1930s they became still freer during the war. Alice points out that all the Services' Clubs she knew were run jointly by men and women. One in particular, in Salisbury, where there were a lot of American officers, actually led to the formation of a joint branch, until a directive from the two central executive committees put a stop to it – and to any enthusiasm the men had had for the movement. At that time it was unconstitutional for women to become members of Toc H – but the barriers were not just legal. The men were generally friendly and courteous, but many women of that generation speak of men's 'fear' of the opposite sex. They were also concerned about orthodoxy: the women's approach was frequently criticised for not being 'right' and their reverence was deemed insufficient. One disagreement arose, remembers Elisabeth Worth, because the women produced a tea towel ('a real money-spinner'), which bore a picture of the lamp; and the men were horrified by the idea of washing up with the beloved Toc H symbol of unity and remembrance. 'I can understand all this', says Alice. 'They go back to the early days, you see, when all these rules and regulations were laid down.' She is not alone in feeling that the women have been held back by the men since the merging of the two organisations in 1971.

Nevertheless, Alice believes that the real mistake was that the two organisations joined so *late*. When she was working in Germany immediately after the war she set up joint groups – and when she told the young men and women in them that back in England they would have to attend separate branches 'they roared with laughter and they said "You tell us we're a family!" ' Although not alone in its policy (she points out that the YMCA and YWCA are still distinct organisations), she is convinced Toc H lost a lot of credibility in this way. 'They should have joined after the war, when they were used to mucking in together. It was the women who had kept Toc H going.'

There are numerous examples of this special contribution the women made. Crutched Friars, the headquarters of the LWH, was found to contain a crypt which was big enough to serve as an air raid shelter for large numbers of people from the tenement buildings on the east side of Tower Hill. Every night a couple of residents of the house, or of the other LWH hostel nearby, were on duty to serve tea and biscuits; but as well as conversation, concerts and films were soon on offer. In Farnborough, LWH opened a club especially for women in the services which was to be the first of many. And one of the most remarkable of their initiatives was a rest home for sailors in the Orkneys. This was run by Alison Macfie at the specific request of Tubby Clayton.

Clayton himself came into his own in these settings. One of Alice's most vivid memories is of a visit he made to the club in Plymouth: 'I absolutely marvelled at this man and the way he talked to those men. He was wonderful with men. He just roamed among the tables talking to them, raising their morale.' This was, of course, the business they were all about. The clubs were successful and extremely popular and were, in Alice's view, particularly good examples of Toc H work: 'They had something specific to do, you see. And there was always such fun. Lots of leg-pulling, making people feel welcome and that the war wasn't on and that they were going to be all right. When bad news came through you helped. They were great places for helping people . . . that was the chief thing I think – just getting to know people and helping people.'

Since Toc H was born in a wartime club for soldiers it is not surprising that it should have run Services' Clubs during the Second World War. What is surprising is the scale of the Toc H war effort. In the year leading up to D-Day there were 300 Toc H clubs in the UK, with some 30,000 voluntary helpers. In one four-week period in 1943, 3,729,687 meals were served and 19,600 beds occupied. There were 120 clubs in the war areas overseas, run by 226 members of staff and a further 100 seconded servicemen. The clubs ranged from a small canteen in a Toc H branch hut or church hall to St Stephen's Club in Westminster, which provided accommodation for men travelling through London on their way to or from leave. Overseas some of the settings were even more extraordinary – one was situated in a three ton truck which travelled with the troops through Burma.

Frank Field, a member of the Toc H war services' staff, described this in 1944:

> We are living with a workshops unit at the moment and find them extremely helpful; things miraculously appear when needed! The lads appreciate the set-up very much indeed and like the table-cloths and cushions; in fact when they saw the curtains which we rigged up to look as though we really had windows, they did not believe it. Our library is well-used, and so far we are running something every night. We have a tent as a quiet room, and the lorry as a reading and activities clubroom – the sides open up and we add on a tarpaulin to make quite a large room. As we have real deck chairs, with arm rests, you can guess that it is soon filled!
>
> So far I have used the back of the truck and the bonnet of a jeep as a stage, working by hurricane lamp and with a wireless set to amplify the portable gramophone. Three-hundred candlepower lamps give a good light for the club-room and quizzes and tombola are popular; tonight they have asked for a spelling bee. We have a full and varied programme for all comers. It gets dark here before 6 p.m., so that the evenings can be very long, and a quiet place to read and write in comfort is very much appreciated. We

> are to be allowed forward with our unit as it goes into action and shall always be just within reach of most of them.

It was a far cry from Plymouth; but essentially, this club was meeting the same needs. It was creating, as had Talbot House in Poperinge, a touch of home, a place to escape for a little from the monotony and discomfort of war, a place to find both friendship and privacy. But the truck in Burma was by no means the most extraordinary setting for this essential Toc H wartime work.

6

In Changi Gaol

In March 1941 the *Toc H Journal* published the first list of members held prisoner in Germany. Already the first news of Toc H groups formed in German PoW camps had filtered through to headquarters in London. In one camp, for instance, Toc H members, who numbered about 100, collected clothing, toilet requisites and cigarettes both for newly arrived prisoners, many of whom had nothing but the clothes they stood up in, and also for Russian prisoners who received no Red Cross parcels.

But not until the war ended was it known that there were also Toc H groups in Japanese PoW camps. Frank Miles, who joined Toc H in Changi gaol in Singapore, and eventually became chairman of the branch there, showed me with quiet pride the minute books and other mementoes that he has carefully preserved for 45 years. As he spoke in matter-of-fact tones about the horrors and privations of those years it was hard to imagine how this gentle man, who in his retirement spends much of his time painting, had come through, not just without becoming hard and cynical, but with a strengthened belief in the power of human beings to create a fairer and better world.

Frank sailed from England in December 1941, believing he was headed for the Middle East. It was while spending Christmas in Cape Town that he learned that the Japanese had entered the war and that his troopship was going to the Far East. As they approached Singapore they saw planes coming towards them and thought at first that it was the RAF coming to welcome them. 'That was the end of the party. That was when we discovered for the first time that the navy had left, the air force had left. We were just a sacrifice to fortune.' The boat docked just 10 days before

Singapore fell. As a stores clerk Frank was one of the last to go ashore. His unit had only just completed setting up a depot when they were ordered to burn it. 'We were told by a warrant officer to disperse, it was a case of every man for himself. But we were strangers to the island. We had no idea where we were.' He and a friend decided that if they walked along the railway line they'd come to Singapore station. 'We thought there'd be another Dunkirk, the navy would get us. It was a shambles, a real shambles. After two or three days we went into a sort of campaign. It was too ridiculous for words. We'd had no training. You can imagine the condition we were in when we were taken prisoner.' On the march to his first prison camp he collapsed.

> Some days in my life are missing. I never worried about it until two or three years ago; but I collapsed in one place and came to in another. I know I must have been some days unconscious. The doctor said: 'You've got a serious illness to fight, without drugs and without proper food. But you're six feet tall and I'd have to use a microscope to see the virus that's causing the illness. Just think of it that way and you'll get through it.' I got through it by reciting as much as I could of Gray's Elegy. And file numbers! I'd been a town hall filing clerk and I recited all the file numbers. When the crunch comes these corny and silly things do keep you going. They give you something to latch on to. It wasn't the big, beefy people, the people who were healthy all the time, who got through so much as the people who were used to having a little illness to contend with, who perhaps hadn't had life so easy.

And he was, as he says, 'lucky'. His illness meant that he wasn't fit enough to go on the working parties sent upcountry to build the notorious railway where so many died. But much of his first two years in captivity was spent in hospital. 'By the time we came home I was really feeling better than I'd felt at any time during imprisonment. It made it much easier for coming home and getting down to things.'

Sitting in his comfortable home in Norfolk, surrounded by prints by his favourite painter, Russell Flint, it's hard to imagine the conditions under which he then lived. Once out of hospital he was in the civilian gaol at Changi. There were four people in a cell built for one.

> You had a concrete slab in the middle that was the bed, with a shape for the head. You'd have one sleeping on the top (he was the lucky one), one on the floor each side and one at the end. You were touching one another, of course. You were touching the walls. And the bugs! They just came at you at night. The only way you got them out of your belongings was to get your belongings into the sun. They crawled out in the heat and you trod on them. That was the only way of keeping them down. Of course, the people who went upcountry had it very much worse.

Quite early on one of his friends, a man from the same unit, escaped with three others. 'I'd no idea he was going to try. He'd been brought up in the Far East, knew the language. If anybody stood a chance it was him.' But they were given away and brought back to Changi after being knocked about. 'He didn't think they'd ever get out of it. He came to see me in the hospital the night before they took him away. It staggers me even now. He came to commiserate with me, to try and cheer *me* up. Next morning he was taken away and shot.'

The diet was mainly rice. Occasionally there were tiny fish, like whitebait, practically no meat and very few vegetables, though they tried to grow some in the prison compound. 'It was surprising what they could do with rice after a time. They played about with it, made it into imitation bread for example.' But it was polished rice, of the lowest grade, and contained no vitamins. Somehow they got hold of the husks from a rice factory floor. These were ground down and stirred in water. 'You've never seen such a horrid mixture in your life, like trying to drink gravel.' But they had to force it down for the vitamins. 'You were on parade and there was no ducking that can. You had to go up and drink it on the spot.'

They were hungry all the time ('I got down to seven stone and then I stopped weighing myself') and talked constantly of food. 'You never dreamt of the high-falutin' stuff. Bread and butter was what I wanted most. For years afterwards I had to go to a lot of dinners. It was a problem to sit down to a four or five course meal. It's funny how we've got traditions that make us do rather silly things. Basically it's stupid to have a four or five course meal. The body doesn't want it, you're only lumbering it with something that it should never have.'

Frank was introduced to Toc H by a friend when he finally moved from hospital into Changi gaol. Having worked as a committee clerk before the war 'it wasn't all that long before I found myself the secretary'. In the peculiar circumstances of Changi gaol Toc H made, Frank believes, three significant contributions. Firstly, it encouraged people to visit those in hospital and try to maintain their morale. The combination of poor diet, heat and overcrowding meant that everyone was subject to recurrent debilitating bouts of dysentery and malaria – though malaria was so common and so frequent that it came to be regarded much as we regard a cold.

Secondly, the weekly Toc H meeting was one of the ways in which men tried to keep their minds alert, to preserve their sanity and their hopes for the future. Each week someone, usually one of the members but occasionally a guest, spoke about his particular area of knowledge or experience. 'I remember a chemist spoke to us about the future of plastics and we thought he was barmy; but of course it's all come about.' It was while preparing a talk on the future of health care that Frank became a fervent believer in the need for a national health service, and that belief determined the course of his future career.

At Changi, unlike the German PoW camps, officers and men were in the same gaol, though in separate accommodation. The third contribution which Toc H made was that it was 'the one place where people of all ranks mixed'. For the last year in captivity, although the members included officers up to the rank of Lt-Colonel, Frank, who 'never got promoted beyond private', was the chairman.

Toc H meetings were held in the chapel, where many of the members also attended Sunday worship. Access to the chapel was never barred, even at times of tension when movement around the camp was severely restricted. At one time all singing was prohibited but the ban was not applied to hymns in chapel. Frank, like many others, slipped into the chapel when he could. 'What you valued at times more than anything else was solitude and the chapel was a quiet corner.

You were in another little world there. It helped to keep the spirit going.'

By 1944 the long retreat which began with the fall of Singapore in February 1942 was over, and the British army was fighting its way south through Burma, on the first stage of the road to Japan. As the advance continued into 1945 the prisoners in Changi gaol were aware, through hidden radio sets, of the progress of the allied forces. The minutes of the Toc H branch, during these last months, convey a strong sense of having made history. At every meeting they discussed preparations for ensuring that the minute book and other records, and the Lamp which had been made in prison, would get safely back to England. Frank undertook to run 'a correspondence club for the interchange of news between members who will be widely scattered'; and he is still in touch with some of those who shared the experience of Toc H in Changi with him.

There's a footnote to the story of Toc H in Changi. In 1988 a television company invited a group of veterans to return to Singapore to make a TV programme, to be broadcast on Channel 4, about their wartime experiences. Frank was unable to go but a fellow-member, Wally Hammond, made the journey. 'I realised', he says, 'that I was being asked to do a job for posterity.' While there the veterans worked with the Singapore Tourist Promotion Board to create a permanent memorial to those who had been imprisoned on the island during the Second World War. Wally presented the Lamp, made in prison, which had been the symbol of the Toc H branch there. It is now displayed in a glass case to remind visitors of what the human spirit can achieve, even in the most inhuman conditions. 'It is very satisfying', says Wally, 'to know it has returned to its original home.'

7

Working with Leprosy

Robin Dunford's first visit to a leprosy settlement was a 'shattering experience'. It was 1944 and he was a green young airforceman serving in Rhodesia. He had joined Toc H there and his 'job' was to organise welfare parcels to go to leprosy colonies throughout the country. He decided he wanted to see for himself what sort of places these were. It was a piece of curiosity which deeply influenced his life.

The first shock was that he found he was expected to stay with one of the patients; the second was that the patient came from Banstead. This was Robin's part of the country and he had often cycled through the town. It literally 'brought home' to him the devastating nature of leprosy. But he also learnt about the widespread misconceptions associated with the disease – the most common strain is not infectious, but does cause grotesque disfigurement.

The Toc H connection with leprosy relief work had begun some 15 years before, when Tubby Clayton stumbled across the disease almost by accident when he was travelling around West Africa. While he was staying near Kano – a large, impressive Muslim protectorate – he made the acquaintance of the local medical officer who also happened to be a Toc H member. He was about to make his first official inspection of the leper colony on the outskirts of the city and Clayton decided to join him.

They were appalled by what they found.

> Here there were human beings without hope [wrote Clayton later] some without limbs and many of them blind. I, who had never hitherto beheld a leper in my life, now saw a nightmare laid out before me under the unrelenting menace of the sun. Some of them gasped and cried aloud

> for water. Others were like the witches in Macbeth stirring their evening meal; women among them clutched enfeebled children close to their breasts. From that time onward leprosy became a nightmare in my mind without redress . . .*

By the time he left Africa he had seen some 30 more leper colonies – he had learned that there *was* hope, and had come to see leprosy relief work as a Christian crusade. One station run by the Church Missionary Society some 80 miles south-west of Kano provided a particularly marked contrast to the hellish scenes he had first encountered:

> There I found calm and order prevailing; respect for patients, treatment to be had, cleanliness reinforced by explanation, as part and parcel of the whole ideal. One felt that here was a strong tradition which heightened the morale of every patient – here was the God of Love in operation, touching in tenderness these hideous sores, and lending sanctity to the whole scene.*

On the voyage home he met one Dr Macdonald and his wife, who had leased land from the chief at Itu in Nigeria and had founded a leper colony there. The meeting was a fateful one. Clayton was deeply impressed by the account they gave him of their work and still more by three letters they showed him, which they had received from patients who had been cured. 'Each of these letters had a deep effect', he wrote to the couple almost 20 years later, 'for they ascribed their rescue directly to our Lord and Saviour.'*

The very night after his return to London, when he was addressing a Toc H meeting in Stepney, Clayton became so carried away as he talked about the disease that he made a completely unplanned plea for volunteers to train and then offer five years to work with those suffering from leprosy in Africa. Six months later, 50 people had volunteered and Toc H had presented BELRA – the British Empire Leprosy Relief Association – with £25,000. One of these volunteers later wrote to Clayton describing the work he was learning to do

*These quotations are reproduced from Tresham Lever's *Clayton of Toc H*, published by John Murray (1971), with kind permission.

and the horrifying extent of the disease which threatened, he believed, to take the country over completely: 'Undoubtedly', he added, 'Toc H has taken up one of the finest pieces of work since the abolition of slavery.'

The connections between Toc H and BELRA were to remain extremely close for many years, as Robin Dunford discovered when he returned to England in 1946. After his experiences abroad he knew he would not be content to continue for long as an auditor in London; but he was astonished, shortly after he got back, to receive a letter from Alec Churcher, who was on the Toc H headquarters staff, asking him to go to see him. He was still more astonished when Churcher showed him a letter he had received from a member of the staff in Johannesburg, who had very briefly encountered Robin just before he left. 'Sometimes', he wrote, 'he gave me the impression that he was wanting to go into the Anglican Church; other times that he wanted to do youth work in England; other times that he wanted to come back overseas and work in leprosy relief. Will you please see him because he is worrying me.'

A year later, Robin was on his way to Nigeria. Alec Churcher – 'a very knowledgeable man' – would have been able to help Robin pursue any of his three options. But the very afternoon that they first met, he took him to see the General Secretary of BELRA, whose office was a stone's throw away from his own. 'Arthur was another Toc H member so we got on like a house on fire and before I knew where I was I knew that this was what I was going to do.'

Robin was to remain in Nigeria for 12 years, working in three different leprosy stations. The first was Itu, the one founded by Dr Macdonald. Here he was principally concerned with the agricultural and industrial aspects of what was a virtually self-sufficient community. One of the ideas behind sending out volunteers like him was that they would be able to take care of the non-medical aspects of running a settlement and free the doctors and nurses to get on with what they were trained for. But inevitably, *everybody* became infected by the eagerness to find and use new treatments. Since 1929, when the colony was founded, the main treatment had been by the subcutaneous injection of a natural oil. But now there was talk of new sulphone drugs from the United

States, which were just starting to make an appearance in Nigeria, and which were said to produce extraordinary results. Subsequently it turned out that there were unfortunate reactions to sulphone treatment and it has long been superseded by more effective therapy. Nevertheless, 'those were dramatic days in which to be involved in leprosy relief work': in an average year they discharged 300 people; in the first year of using the new drug, the figure was 960.

There were other ways in which the treatment was changing at that 'exciting time'. When Robin went to manage a leprosy station in Northern Nigeria later on, they had just begun seeing a few people in outpatient clinics. By the time he left, there were 11 such clinics at distances of up to 1000 miles from the health centre, treating 2500 people.

It was also a time of significant social and political change – Nigeria was to achieve independence in 1960. Robin's work was physically demanding and he was on duty from dawn until dusk and on call 24 hours a day. He had no time for politics and was not called on to take a stand; he and his colleagues were seen as fitting in somewhere between the government and the missions and as belonging to neither. It was not until he was back in England, at the time of the Biafran War (1967–70), that Robin developed 'active' political views as a result of hearing a friend of his speak disparagingly about 'those Ibos'. 'And I wouldn't have this at all, you see – it made me far more political and politically aware because I felt he was being so unfair.'

But in fact his convictions had been building up over the years as he had witnessed a succession of minor but humiliating injustices inflicted on the black people of Africa. The races never mixed on terms of equality; patterns of status and the divisions of labour were clear and unquestioned. He recalls watching a 'poor white' labourer standing on a ladder to paint a fence and handing down his brush to an African who was waiting at the bottom of the ladder to do his, more menial, task – dipping the paintbrush into the paint. On another occasion, Robin and others in the Toc H group on the RAF station decided to build a hut for themselves. 'The very idea of white men doing any manual work was foreign. Everyone thought we were mad, but we thought it was great fun!' Even sickness was no leveller. The man from Banstead was one of only five white sufferers on the leprosy station. There were 200 blacks – and all the doctors were white.

He was startled to see his own daughter, born in 1954, become bossy and adopt 'the superior white attitude' by the time she was four; 'she was a kind of natural. It was really quite extraordinary to see'. He was glad to move to England with her to a society less damaging to human dignity; and he gradually came to see that racism corrupted the oppressor as much as the oppressed. When he left Rhodesia at the end of the war and was walking down the streets of Durban towards the boat, the Africans got up from the pavement to let him pass. Just a few months later, 'I was walking down the streets of Lagos and *I* had to go into the gutter to let the Africans pass. I used to say at one time that I thought the Lagos situation was a far healthier one than the Durban one because ultimately, no matter how you looked at it, the country belonged to the African people. But I'm not sure now it was so healthy – there was a lack of consideration either way for *people*.'

Robin's attitude was always slightly unconventional. Even in his Rhodesian days he was always keen to have as much contact as possible with Africans and he achieved this mainly through his church (he was licensed as a lay preacher in Matabeleland). But it never occurred to him or to any of the members of Toc H there that their 'mixture' should extend so far. This was not because they lacked originality or courage. Robin and the other members of the Toc H group in RAF Mount Hampden broke one very powerful taboo on several occasions, when they invited some Italian prisoners of war to spend an evening with them, listening to Italian operatic recordings in the Toc H hut. 'We were slated for that, but we felt that it was a good thing to do.' There were numerous other traditional barriers to be broken down and both this group, and the one in Salisbury, brought together people who were widely different in age, background and belief. His very introduction to the Toc H group was indicative of its flavour:

> . . . two airman in beds on either side of mine used to wage a political battle of words in the evenings, quite literally over the top of me. Their battle was fierce and unceasing

> in those non-working hours, except for Tuesday evenings. On Tuesday evenings it was quite different, as there seemed to be an agreed 'ceasefire'; they got ready, and went off amicably together to some unspecified destination, for some unspecified purpose. I was curious and, eventually, my curiosity got the better of me. So one Tuesday evening I asked, as innocently as possible, 'Where are you off to then?' The reply I received was more direct than I had expected. 'If you're really interested, perhaps you'd like to come with us.' That was how I attended my first traditional Toc H branch meeting and how I came into Toc H membership.

Religious barriers were also broken down. 'It was here', Robin subsequently wrote, 'that I learned the joy of praying with men who seldom, if ever, would be seen in a Christian place of worship.' Robin denies being 'a spiritual person' but 'I acknowledge the spiritual in me. Prayer is important to me . . . it teaches me how to live.' Ritual, however, and denominational allegiance, he finds irrelevant and even damaging.

His suspicion of ritual and tradition has made him at times a controversial figure within Toc H. His extensive and continuing contact with young people has convinced him that a misguided exclusivist interpretation of the Christian basis of Toc H is putting them off and damaging the movement as a whole. Despite differences in language and format, he argues, 'all the old magic of the Toc H of the past – the friendship, the service, the fairmindedness and the witness; all the fun and excitement of discovery; and certainly all the ideology and spirituality – still work within Toc H today', and he longs for these aspects to be developed in a way appropriate for this generation. For then, he believes, the movement's Christian heritage could be transformed and more truly lived out.

At the moment, he feels that many young people are missing out by refusing to accept the Fourth Point of the Toc H Compass, which calls on members to acknowledge the spiritual nature of man and to test the Christian way of life by trying it out. But the older generation is also guilty of separating the Fourth Point from the other three: 'I would say we have failed because we have left all that sort of thing to the padres.' The four go together, no one is the preserve of the expert, and only if they are all integrated can a complete life be hoped for. He believes that Toc H's recognition of this is, or should be, one of the things that distinguishes it from other organisations. There are those who are appalled at Robin's refusal to demand commitment to the language and traditions which have sustained members for so much of Toc H's history, and his argument that even a traditional Christian allegiance is not necessary to Toc H membership; they feel that he and those who share his views are 'watering down' the Christian message of Toc H. 'They're not really looking at what we're trying to *do*', is his response. 'What was Jesus Christ doing? He was showing a way in which one *got relationships right* – with other people, with yourself and with God.'

It is this which he believes Toc H has taught him. 'It has', he says quite simply, 'enabled me to be myself.' As long as Toc H is providing people with this opportunity it is fulfilling its function, even if it is not following any recognisable formula. He insists that individuals can carry out the work of Toc H in unexpected ways and that it is a positive thing if a person decides to move on when they feel restricted within it, to take what they have learned elsewhere. During all his years in Nigeria he remained a member of his home branch in Epsom, because they, and he, felt that he was doing a Toc H job there although he was working for another organisation.

When he returned to England he did become very involved in Toc H, both in the Midlands (where he moved to) and nationally. Professionally, he continued with LEPRA, as the post-colonial charity was named, working for several years in the publicity and fund raising departments, before moving on to become a qualified social worker at the age of 45. Now, in his retirement, he 'lives' Toc H to such an extent that he and his wife, who is active in the Church, find they have to book in an evening a week in their diaries to be together.

He no longer has any particular involvement with leprosy relief work and nor does Toc H, although a number of branches still raise money for LEPRA. For many years Toc H retained a couple of places on that charity's management committee, but this has now ceased by mutual agreement. Toc H's work with leprosy has been a remarkable example of its ability to respond, sometimes with dramatic effectiveness, to a particular need. It was typical of Clayton's capacity to inspire concern and practical commitment beyond all probability. To Robin Dunford, it seems a bit of an anomaly that so much energy was dedicated to this one cause when there were so many other needs around. 'Tubby went at it hook, line and sinker and sold it so completely to the movement that in some places the branches were spending so much time doing leprosy fund raising that they weren't really Toc H branches any more, just extensions of leprosy relief work.' But part of the process was to withdraw gracefully when the time was right, to leave others to continue a specific task while Toc H continued with the business of promoting the Four Points.

This withdrawal is an entirely right and proper attitude and it is built into the Toc H ethos, argues Robin. Almost every piece of work the movement undertakes should eventually be handed on, although there is, he thinks, one exception. Friendship circles, with which he is deeply involved, and which we look at in a later chapter, depend on the Toc H philosophy and approach to people in a way which most other forms of 'service' do not. For their success depends not on funds or technology or research or even on dedication – but on the building of 'right relationships' which enable people 'to be themselves'.

8

A Malaysian Ghost

Like many others Frank Field has apparently moved far from Toc H; but he doesn't see it like that. All his journeys, to Malaysia, to India, to Hong Kong and Taiwan, he has seen as a response to the original inspiration he found in Eastbourne in the 1930s and in his wartime work for Toc H in Burma. In his retirement he has returned to Eastbourne and rejoined the faithful remnant of the Toc H branch.

Only the deeply tanned face gives any hint of his extraordinary past. There are no mementoes of his travels on display in his flat. He talks, for the most part, in a quiet, self-deprecating manner, as though anxious to play down the drama of his life as a travelling Mr Fixit. Now in his late seventies, he remains tall, straight-backed and powerfully built. Though he speaks quietly his opinions are expressed firmly and humorously. He seems an enviably happy man.

After his wartime experiences in Burma he returned to Eastbourne. In partnership with a friend, he started a market garden which prospered; but he couldn't really settle. He had been exposed to other races and cultures and increasingly he longed to go back to the East. One day he happened to read an article about the emergency in Malaysia and the need to win the hearts and minds of the people. He volunteered to help, was invited for an interview and two weeks later he was on his way to Malaysia.

'You'll probably laugh at this', said Frank. 'What we were doing was locking people up in villages, taking away their freedom and teaching them democracy.' The idea was to round up all the people who were squatting illegally, and put them behind barbed wire so that the communist insurgents couldn't get to them. Then new village communities had to be established, schools and clinics built, village committees established. Frank was assigned to a team responsible for creating 13 villages. 'I was the only one with the basic training – and the heart – to get into this sort of thing, and within a very few months I found myself chief resettlement officer for a vast area. We had 10% of the total problem in our district.'

But if the work was exciting it was also extremely dangerous. After about a year 'it got so bad, I was being ambushed or shot at at meetings or generally chased around, three times in 10 days. This wasn't so bad for me – well, it was not happy for me – but you see you'd got staff and they could be got at. It wasn't fair on them, so they pushed me off up country.' He was near Penang, building another five villages and developing youth work, for three 'very happy' years.

When Frank left Malaysia, just before independence, he made another attempt to settle down, this time near Darwin, in the Northern Territory of Australia. He took a plot of land, built a house and became a pineapple farmer. He was, he says, happily settled in Australia when he suddenly heard from Harry Haines, who had worked with him in Malaysia and was now working for the World Council of Churches. They had an apparently insoluble problem, but Haines thought Frank could help to solve it for them. Following the partition of India in 1947 refugees fleeing from East Bengal (later to become Bangladesh) had settled at one of the main railway stations in Calcutta. Some 15 years later they were still there. The government, the railway authorities, the police, everyone concerned wanted to shift them, but no one had been able to. Now a group of American church people had visited Calcutta, been appalled by what they'd seen and raised a large sum of money. 'Harry Haines had an insoluble problem and the money to solve it; but nobody to do the job. So he asked if I could come for three months and start it off. I told him that three months was no good to anybody. I'd come out and do the job.'

I wondered how one would start to cope with a problem which everyone had, for years, agreed to be insoluble. 'It was just a confidence trick,' said Frank, 'a matter of persuading people you could do it and then getting them to do it themselves.' Once the politicians were persuaded, the government gave a piece of land. Once the railway authorities were persuaded, they provided transport. Students at the engineering college designed low cost houses and taught the people how to build them. 'I got everybody into the act and built three villages.' The building of the villages provided the people with work. But building the community was as important as erecting houses. He formed committees, established scout troops, in other words did what he'd done earlier in Malaysia. And, he adds, 'persuaded the people that they'd done it themselves. That was the most important thing.'

The plot of land he'd been allocated was only about four acres, so there was no space for cultivation. 'The better people you found jobs in the army or the police. The rogues you set up in business of some sort' – a phrase which concealed what must have been an immense amount of work, persuading, guiding, with every individual. Sixteen hundred families (about 8000 people) were moved from the station and established in three villages, which still flourish 25 years later.

'Twice', he told me, 'they made me weep.' The first time was while they were still living at the station. A party from Sweden came round and Frank heard them ask why, after all these years, people thought they would move this time. And he heard an old man reply: 'Sir, a man has come from God and now I know we shall move.' Some years later he was back in the area and went to a service at the cathedral. 'I saw a group of people at the back who were looking at me. I didn't recognise them at all but as I came out they came and knelt and asked for a blessing. A hell of a situation. I still weep now.'

He was asked by the World Council of Churches to take on a similar job in Hong Kong, creating a village for refugees and helping to establish a farming co-operative. By then he had something of a reputation as a troubleshooter and he was sent to Taiwan to sort out the problems of a village which, according to Frank, 'had been built by an idiot'. This sounded like another impossible job: he didn't know the country; he didn't know the language; and he could only be spared from his job in Hong Kong for two weeks.

He went first to the committee in Taipeh, who were responsible for the project. The bishop, who had only recently arrived and was determined to sort out the problems, asked him what he was going to do. 'I'll produce a rabbit', he said. 'They think I'm a magician, so they'll expect to see a rabbit.'

In other words, as in Calcutta, he would have to pull off a 'confidence trick'.

He went to the village, found someone to interpret for him, and spoke to as many people as he could about the problems as they saw them. Then he returned to the committee and simply reported what he'd heard. He expressed no view of his own, simply told them the problems as the people of the village had expressed them. That was enough to bring home to the committee the size of the problem and the need to do something about it. Everyone began talking at once – 'just like a hive of bees'. And then he had to return to his job in Hong Kong. He never did hear what happened in the end.

It's impossible to say how much of his approach to his work came from what he learnt in his early years in Toc H and how much was due to his own idiosyncratic personality. Toc H has, however, been a continuing thread through all the variety of experiences that have come to him in different parts of the world. It has been, in a sense, his extended family. He never married. Until his retirement he had no permanent home. He has had lots of acquaintances but few intimate friends. But, despite all his travelling, he never lost touch with Toc H and when he finally returned to Eastbourne he rejoined the branch. It seems to have little to offer him. Where there were once two branches in Eastbourne, each with over 40 members, there is now one with just five members, all of them well past retirement age. There is no longer the challenge and excitement of the early years but it remains his family. And you don't leave a family.

There's something else that's central to Frank's personality, as to so many people who have been, in one way or another, touched by Toc H, and that's a unique and individual approach to religion. He recalled one powerful, and still vivid, religious experience from his time in Australia. 'I've been to about every kind of religious meeting you can imagine', he said. 'I've been to every sort of church or temple or shrine or what-have-you but I've never ever – except in the most unlikely place – felt the presence of God.'

That most unlikely place was the prison in Darwin. One Christmas he and another prison visitor were asked to get the mess hall ready for the Midnight Mass. From a room off the hall they watched 'shadowy figures' coming from their cells for the service. 'When the little bell rang for the Elevation of the Host the whole place was lit, suffused with a warm, yellow glow, as if someone had turned up a light. It took three or four minutes to go off again. I've never ever had such an experience anywhere else. Quite incredible. That's the last place you'd expect something like that. Quite incredible.'

When he talks about Malaysia he insists that life there is on a different level, a different plane of existence. 'You just knew when it was dangerous. You knew exactly how far you could go.' He told me about his assistant Mr Wang, whose wife kept seeing a ghost. Frank went with another assistant to the temple to consult the priest. 'Ah yes', said the priest, 'Today is Monday. My day for talking to the gods is Wednesday. Could you come back Thursday or Friday?' On their return the priest told them that the carpenter who had built the house years before had put some kind of good luck token in the roof. His wife had been pregnant at the time but had later lost the child. Now dead, she was being drawn back by the baby in the womb. Frank was impressed – he hadn't mentioned Mrs Wang's pregnancy. The priest gave him a nicely wrapped little package, telling him to burn it, mix the ashes in water with a particular twig and sprinkle the room. And there was no further haunting. 'It's incredible', said Frank, 'but everybody believes in it and it works.'

He went on to talk about a much more frightening episode, and as he talked his voice became grim. 'I was sleeping in a downstairs room. There was no glass in the windows, but shutters and wire mesh so no one could get in. I was fast asleep. You know how it is when you sense someone there. I woke up and as I woke I sat up in bed. There was a shadow by the dressing table, a sudden bang and I was shot dead. I was dead. I fell back.' After several minutes he realised he was still alive. There was no smell of gunpowder and he was not wounded. Evidently there had been no intruder – or rather, the intruder had been a ghost.

Alongside such experiences goes a profound sense of having been guided throughout his life. 'You see', he said, 'my father was killed when I was seven and I've always had the feeling that "I must be about my father's business". It's very hard to explain this but all my life I've been guided and directed. A door has opened or this has happened and it's flowed. I knew what I was directed to and all the time I followed it it worked. It's been a totally different life from the ordinary, the run of the mill.'

At the same time he's frequently scathing about the conventionally religious. He mentioned, for instance, 'all the old dears who think they're going to heaven to live with Jesus. I wonder if they know that Jesus was a Middle Eastern Arab and if they'd really be happy living with him.' He talked about the missionaries who had a meeting to decide something completely trivial like whether or not to change the lavatory doors. 'They spent all day putting it up to God in prayer.' And he talked about the group who had a long and inconclusive meeting which ended with prayer. 'They turned round to kneel on their chairs and turned their backs on each other. It never occurred to them that this was typical of what they'd been doing throughout the meeting.'

As these comments suggest, Frank is above all a practical man, a problem solver, someone who likes to get things done. I asked him whether, looking back, he could see any one common thread running through all the different work that he had done. Had it something to do with helping people to stand on their own feet? 'Not so much that', he replied. 'That was incidental. Involving people, that was the main thing. People learned how to do things. And had a good time, too. Everybody's involved. It's theirs. This is the thing all the way through. It's theirs. You can occasionally find a photograph of me but it's very rare. And always working with, or usually behind, other people.'

That's still the way he lives his life. Every now and again he invites a boy from the area to spend a day in London with him. He discusses with the boy what they're going to see, gives him timetables and tube maps and leaves him to work out the programme for the day. Then, he says, when the boy has to go to London on his own, he'll know his way about. 'It all helps, and it keeps me young too.'

Perhaps that's why, despite all his remarkable memories, he never gave me the impression of living in the past. Doors are still opening for him. And his enjoyment of life is still infectious.

9

Transition

On D-Day, 6 June 1944, Alice Welford happened to be staying in a Toc H Services' Club for women in Bournemouth:

> It was unexpected and very thrilling. I'd come down the day before and seen all these troops gathering on all these little side roads with tanks and various other things. And I'd arrived at the club and the only place that I could sleep was on a sofa half way up the stairs. I woke in the morning to hear shuffle, shuffle; and I looked out of the window and there was the Canadian Air Force going by down to the loading area for ships and then later on in the day we could hear the guns across the Channel . . . and we watched them all go by during the day – all the Americans and the Canadians and the British . . .

A year or two later, she went out to Germany to work with the Toc H staff team there. She wrote home to the LWH magazine about the suffering and devastation she witnessed:

> There was nothing to be seen except a chaos of desolation, and we picked our way over the bricks to the underground shelter, which is now the home of about 200 men, women and children – a typical home in these great blitzed cities of the Ruhr, of Hanover and Hamburg. Thirty feet underground, on either side of a dingy stone galley, were little cells, windowless and stuffy. In some of these narrow cabins perhaps five people live; here they sleep in bunks and drink their soup (their only food) which they fetch from the communal kitchen; here Mother does the washing and hangs it on a wire to drip on the heads of children sitting reading. The school is down here too; the playground the dingy corridor or the rubble overhead. One young 'widow'

> had colour-washed her stone walls, and hung up some pretty material to curtain off the bunks; her three children were spotlessly clean and neat, as are most German children.
>
> By comparison with these bunkers, the cellars are shocking, for there is no sanitation and often they are damaged and rat-ridden. An aged couple (he was dying) had hung sacking across their room to catch the falling dirt and to keep out the rain; another 'widow' (a woman with a husband missing on the Russian front) suffering from acute hunger oedema, got rid of her waste by emptying it through a hole she had cut in a sewage pipe running past her room. She had her three small children living with her; a Toc H branch is now sending her food parcels . . .

Alice was particularly affected by the plight of the young. Many of the schools had been demolished; equipment and books were scarce, teachers ageing and classes huge. More important still, there were the effects of a previous education to counteract:

> In 1936 the entire youth of Germany was *compelled* to join the Hitler Youth . . . The system was elaborately organised and every detail, even a meetings programme, was imposed from above . . . And now what is to be done with these boys and girls who for years have been told what to believe, and now find that this creed has led to a complete and utter disintegration of their nation? Disillusioned, many of them embittered, hungry and ill-clad, they face a future without hope.

Alice became involved in Anglo-German discussion groups which had been set up by her colleagues, and was convinced that this was a suitable Toc H piece of work. These young people had had plenty of discipline, but no training, as far as she could see, in *relationships*. 'I always get involved with people – it doesn't matter who they are. And I saw a need with all these young people – highly educated in the Nazi sphere but completely at sea when it came to discussions, because they'd never been allowed to do it, you see. They'd had to accept everything. And it was so moving because it was all so new to them.' One young man who joined the staff of one of the clubs shortly after the war, was to remain there, working as the Senior Accountant for Toc H in Germany, for more than 40 years.

Alice returned home to become involved in new ventures – such as 'Dinton Weeks' (holiday and discussion weeks in a large country house) and her first pilgrimage to Talbot House, Poperinge. She also found that it was easy and rewarding to set up new branches in the West Country, largely with the women who had been involved in the Services' Clubs.

In the country as a whole, however, there was some disappointment about how few of those involved so actively during the war became members of Toc H after it was over. Some of those who did show an interest were thoroughly put off by what they found. When Constance Beazley's brother moved near a Toc H branch, he went along – only to discover 'a group of old men talking about what used to be'. He did not go again and found other outlets for his energies and altruism.

There was no shortage of such opportunities. The age of specialised charities was beginning – Toc H itself helped launch BELRA, which later became LEPRA. The idea that the support of the poor and needy was a private duty had given way to the notion of professional care and government responsibility. The welfare state had been born. For some, it was an excuse to wash their hands of those in need; for others it provided a more promising channel for their idealism. Frank Miles had become committed to the idea of the National Health Service when preparing a talk about it for the Toc H club in Changi Gaol. When it was launched in 1948: 'I wanted to go and practise what I'd preached.' His work as an administrator was to take up most of his time, energy and zeal for more than a quarter of a century. Being in at the start was an exciting challenge: 'You'd got nothing but empty filing cabinets. You couldn't go to the files to see what had been done before. Everything you were dealing with was new.'

He did eventually rejoin Toc H – but not until he had retired and had some leisure time once more. This was a common pattern, for there were careers to be built and families to be enjoyed. Even some of the women, who would have been glad of an outlet for both social and creative energies in the 1930s, were now directing these towards careers.

Constance Beazley points out that the women who went out to work during the First World War returned to their homes afterwards; those who did so during the Second, stayed out. And the modern career can be all-consuming – she is struck by how few people of the intellectual and professional classes Toc H attracts today in contrast to the past. These were days of decline, she now thinks – although only in retrospect, looking at the average age of the members today. For the fifties were her heyday and she felt at the time that she was part of a dynamic, exciting movement with real achievements to its name.

In fact, it was above all a time of transition. It was not yet apparent that the changes in society and in the attitudes of the young meant that the details of Toc H's role and methods of work would need to change quite radically if it was to be true to its original and underlying purpose. Not until the 1960s did it really become clear how far Toc H needed to change in order to remain essentially the same.

The breakthrough was the development of 'projects' – a variety of short workcamps aimed at young people. They appealed to a generation which had opportunities and expectations of a sort previously available only to a select few. Independence, education, travel and a career which fulfilled were beginning to be sought as rights and they provided both the background and the impetus to a changing perception of society and of the individual's role within it. 'In the 1960s', says Sue Cumming, who was electrified by her first Toc H project as a teenager:

> We were breaking down the old, accepted, established things of our parents' generation – we were following on from the angry young men of the 1950s who were beginning to challenge them at an intellectual level. 'Respectability' was a swear word. I think it was the beginning of a much greater consciousness of individual choice. And the proof of that is to be seen now, in that most of us ended up making sure we were all right.

Having been inspired by her first project to see life as 'an adventure', Sue went out to East Africa after university, to teach. It was part of the British Government's post independence aid scheme – sending graduates to teach in secondary schools so that more African students achieved the standard of education necessary to become teachers themselves. 'We went out to make ourselves obsolete.'

She had a wonderful time: 'it was the spirit of volunteering at its best.' In her two and a half years she taught everything from 'O' level maths to Scottish country dancing and found herself head of the science department. She recalls above all the fun and the teamwork and the colossal enthusiasm that they all shared. Part of her motivation in going had been a long-standing belief that the most useful way to be a Christian was to *do* things, to offer practical help to those in need. But she shared with many of her contemporaries an attitude to 'doing good' which was subtly different from that of their parents and grandparents. When she came back to England at the end of her contract, she went to her old church to talk about her experiences. One woman praised her for making such a 'wonderful sacrifice' in giving three years of her life to these people. Sue's sharp rejoinder was that the only sacrifice she had made had been in coming back.

The attitude to 'service' had changed. This was a 'generation which had nothing to feel guilty about' as Constance Beazley puts it. Although social problems persist and young people have continued to feel drawn to help those in need: 'they don't think of it as *service*. Some of them in a way have a better attitude because they are saying "here is my brother; I must get alongside him". Much better than what I was brought up to – which was "here we are, we're comfortable and we've got money so we must help the poor".'

An increasing number of organisations and schemes sprang up which enabled young people to 'get alongside' those in need. Jennifer Mitchell had already spent a year teaching in Borneo with VSO by the time she got to Bristol University. Keen to continue some sort of practical voluntary work and put off by the long queue for IVS at the Freshers' Fair she joined the Toc H university group instead. It was VSO, inevitably, which broke open the doors of her perception; but Toc H which enabled her to continue the process in her own country. In retrospect, she sees it as having provided her with an essential antidote to 'the isolation and elitism' of being a student. It balanced the education and set of values she had been given, persuading her that they were too exclusively intellectual and narrowly competitive.

For young people such as Jennifer and Sue, the emphasis on learning which had been integral to Toc H, was an irrelevance. Constance Beazley recalls that for many of her contemporaries, the movement's intellectual component had been a great attraction; but as education has become more widely available and its methods and aims have changed, so Toc H's role in this respect has become redundant. Learning by rote and the mastery of facts have given way to an encouragement of debate in the classroom – Toc H's emphasis on discussion, on 'finding your own convictions while listening with respect to the views of others', is less novel – at least in theory – than it was. Yet she was struck recently when she heard a young man describe Toc H as the only place where he felt he was *listened* to – a sentiment which echoed exactly the words of many women she had known in the 1950s.

The subject which young people find themselves discussing in Toc H with the most unexpected openness and urgency is religion. Many of them find the Christian basis of the movement hard to accept and refuse to pay lip-service to it; this is a great change from the days when even those without an active Christian belief (and there were many) took its presence for granted in the charitable organisation of which they happened to be a part – much as they accepted the role of the Established Church in their nation. When Mary Edwards joined in 1951 at the age of 16, having been brought up with Toc H, she knew simply that it was her ambition to be fully a part of something she enjoyed so much, and did not go into the philosophy in any depth: 'people nowadays tend to think more deeply about the meaning of membership before coming to sign a membership form . . . I'm sure at 16 I didn't even think about it!'

But as time went on, she found that its influence on her understanding of Christianity and on her spiritual development was immense. Like so many others, she valued the opportunity it gave her of doing practical work in the community at a time when 'the Churches were only interested in their own people'. The feeling of being accepted as an individual that she always had in Toc H (even as a child she appreciated the fact that she was always 'Mary' rather than

'Ron and Margaret's little girl'), and the discovery that she was capable of all sorts of things that she had assumed were beyond her, gradually helped her to lose her shyness and to learn to be more at ease with herself and with her conscience. For her, the hardest statement in the Bible has always been the instruction to love your neighbour as yourself: 'I find it very very easy indeed to love my neighbour and I find it terribly difficult to love me because I know me. Toc H helped me to look at how one loves oneself and at the implications of patterning one's life on Christ's.' It did so not just by 'practical Christianity' and by personal support but by issuing challenges to her thinking. She was urged to reflect on her faith and to analyse it in a way that she was never encouraged to do 'in the pew'. The unique contribution of Toc H to certain aspects of religious life has diminished as the Churches themselves have changed. Not only do they now place more emphasis on 'the Social Gospel', they are also increasingly concerned to work together rather than to emphasise their differences. 1942 saw the foundation of the British Council of Churches, which quickly became both respected and influential. Toc H had been pioneering in its ecumenism and numerous people testify to the radical effect that working with those of other denominations and attending their services had on them. Elisabeth Worth had clung on to 'a rather narrow Anglicanism' as one of the few securities in her life. The people she met through Toc H changed her perception so much that she and her husband became active in the ecumenical cause and remain so to this day. But just *because* inter-denominational dialogue and collaboration have become such accepted parts of religious life, and because there are now so many opportunities for both, Toc H finds itself with less of a part to play.

Yet it is in the general area of spiritual exploration, loosely defined, that Toc H does seem to be able to offer something very particular today. Ann Crouch, now in her fifties, had a 'Damascus road experience in reverse' as a young woman which converted her to atheism. Deciding to join Toc H when she became involved in it in the 1970s, wasn't easy:

> An outsider looking at Toc H sees very little difference to any other church group. I couldn't see how on earth I

could overcome that, though I was very much drawn to wanting to join. There's a close-knit warmth in it which is about everyday life and not about church-related activities. Being part of Toc H challenged me to think about where I was, and why I was living, and what I was doing. I see it in terms of being alive and enjoying it, and of how I relate to other people.

Toc H has been important to her in clarifying her thoughts and she believes that she, in turn, has also challenged the organisation to think about its handling of the subjects of spirituality and prayer. She doesn't believe in a God but she does claim to 'follow a Christian way of life'. By this she doesn't just mean that she does 'good works':

I think a lot about where my spirituality lies; my role in life, my role in eternity. That sounds funny if you don't have a concept of life after death; but I do have a concept of eternity. I believe that life is final but the spirit of what I do will live after me whatever happens to my body. That's where the eternal bit comes in. If I visualise it it's as a circular thing which is made up of millions and millions of specks and these specks are specks of life – yours, mine, the leaf on that tree, the bird over there, the nits in someone's hair . . . You're part of a much larger entity. You're both very tiny and at the same time very real and necessary. To me the sacred part is to do with life itself so that even the greenfly on my plants have a right to live.

The Churches are still failing many who want to make their own spiritual journey rather than enclose themselves in walls of dogma. In 1989, the Central Council of Toc H accepted a statement reaffirming the Christian basis of Toc H in contemporary language, and indicating its intention to respond to this need. The National Chaplain of the movement, Alan Johnson, was one of its architects and believes that although it does not contain any change of principle it does represent a distinct shift of *balance*:

In the very early days, Toc H provided what the Church did not in that it provided social service. That was the key then, because society was, at least in word, very Christian. I think Toc H, and society, have changed now. We're not

> experts at 'doing things' and I don't think we should be. But what we should be expert at is enabling the meetings to take place and the discovery of soul in the process of meeting. I think society needs *that* more than it did 75 years ago.

This means that the movement must remain 'in the middle but not on the fence' – clearly asserting both its Christian inspiration and its openness to all. And the experiences of Ann Crouch and of young people such as Liz Jones, now in her twenties, suggest that it is succeeding in this. When Liz went on her first project she was 'at that stage you go through. I thought of myself as being a slightly cynical person. I liked to call myself an atheist because I thought it sounded like a good word. Toc H was good because it made me start thinking about that, deciding, well, there's more to it than that.' What really fascinated her was that certain people she met seemed to have 'some kind of aura about them, a kind of serenity. I wanted to find out why it was there. And it seemed that why it was there was a lot to do with matters of a spiritual or religious nature.'

The 'cynicism' Liz had espoused – and often in a more profound and permanent form – is common in Britain as it enters the last decade of the twentieth century. Despite the sweeping changes in structures and assumptions that society has seen since the Second World War – in many cases more rapid and far-reaching than those which followed the First – there remains an underlying separation and suspicion between people. Tubby Clayton had spoken of the need to work for the 'reconciliation of man with man and of man with God'. As Toc H struggled to continue that essential task in the years following the Second World War, it found itself beset by unexpected difficulties. But it was also to be taken by surprise by unpredicted successes and delights.

10

A School of Peace

The story of Toc H has taken us to many place, to Changi, to Nigeria, to Malaysia, but Belgium, where it all began, is a continuing strand in the tale. When the First World War ended Talbot House in Poperinge was handed back to its owner, the hop dealer, its job apparently done. But as people came together to give peacetime form to what they had learned they began to dream of regaining possession of Talbot House. In 1929, through the generosity of Lord Wakefield of Hythe, this became possible. An Anglo-Belgian Talbot House Association was formed to take responsibility for it. The chapel furniture, which had been used in Mark I, returned to the Upper Room. Many of the notices, which had been carefully preserved through the intervening years, returned to the walls. A brick house, with baths and toilets, was built in the garden, a wash-house so magnificent that the legend grew up that the Belgian builder had read metres where the English architect had intended feet. The man responsible for overseeing the work was Paul Slessor and so, with the love of nicknames typical of the period, the new building became known as the Slessorium. It is so called to this day, though with the installation of toilets and showers in the main house it no longer retains its original purpose.

Veterans of the Great War wanted to return to Flanders, to visit the graves of their friends and to commit themselves anew to building a better world. But Talbot House was never intended to be solely a base for pilgrimages by old soldiers. Nor was it to be a museum. The first handbook for visitors, published in 1930, said that it was 'a training place, made more significant by the immense background of the Salient, a place where young Toc H members, the likely leaders of the future, may come for conference, inspiration, refreshment of mind and spirit'. That remains its purpose 60 years on.

But in 1940 fighting returned to Belgium. There were dreams of re-opening Talbot House in Poperinge for its original purpose. The rapid advance of the German armies soon ended those dreams and five members of the Toc H staff, including Rex Calkin, the General Secretary, and Austen Williams, later to become widely known as the vicar of St Martin's in the Fields in London, were captured.

Several British soldiers as they fled to Dunkirk saw, or thought they saw, Talbot House in ruins, damaged or destroyed by German shells. One man even claimed to have searched in the rubble and to have unearthed a pair of candlesticks. There was no communication with occupied Belgium and no definite news could be obtained. Philip Clayton argued that it would be the sacred duty of Toc H to rebuild the house exactly as it had been. Barclay Baron, the editor of the *Toc H Journal*, wrote in response that the house, even if it had survived, would have less significance for succeeding generations. 'To us it was experience, memory, real life; to them it is history, hearsay, tradition.' It would be 'increasingly hard to interpret it without false sentiment'. Nearly 50 years on, experience has proved him wrong. The house speaks powerfully to people who were not yet born when he wrote those words. Yet he may well have been right when he said that the house rebuilt as a facsimile 'would have no real meaning at all'. In any event, after several months of uncertainty news came, in a letter from the Belgian caretakers to Rex Calkin in his German PoW camp, that the house had survived unharmed.

When allied forces returned to the continent the first Toc H member to re-enter Talbot House in Poperinge, in September 1944, was BBC war correspondent Frank Gillard. 'One week of hard work', he reported, 'by half a dozen willing cleaners and the whole place will be as immaculate as ever.' Toc H now began to hear for the first time the story of how the people of Poperinge had, at great risk, preserved the contents of the house through the years of German occupation.

Jeanne Oreel-Battheu, who as a child had known Talbot House during the First World War, still lived in Poperinge, as she does today. The German authorities, she says, gave 24 hours notice of their intention of taking over the house. That night four men came, with a horse and cart, and everything in the house was removed. The smaller objects were hidden in attics and cupboards in the houses of 'patriots'. All the furniture was stored in a large cellar and screened by a false wall. The Toc H Lamp was buried in the garden. 'They said, even if they find the things, they will never find our Lamp. Only two people knew where it was.' When the Germans came next morning they found the house completely empty. 'They asked Mr Lahaye (the vice-president of the Talbot House Association) what had happened and he said: "Ah well, the door was left unlocked, and the people here, they have nothing to burn to keep warm." '

The day the Germans left, Jeanne's brother-in-law, Marcel de Rynck-Battheu, decided to go in. 'It was strictly forbidden, of course, because of booby-traps, to go into a house that had just been left by the Jerries' (as she always calls them, even today – the experience of occupation leaves hurts and divisions that do not heal). But Poperinge people, she says, are stubborn and he insisted 'just to have a look. He went into the cellar and there was a bomb there. The whole lounge was burning. When they left they burned all their papers. It would have set the house on fire.' The fire brigade dealt with the fire and the bomb; and then the contents were returned. Everything came back, even a hat left in a cupboard by one of the last English visitors before the war started. It was returned to him with pride when he next visited Poperinge.

In December 1944 Talbot House was re-opened for the many troops in the area at that time. Once again it was thronged with soldiers of different ranks and many nationalities – the congregation at one service in the Upper Room included a Czech chaplain and six Chinese soldiers. There were 10 Poperinge women, including Jeanne and her sister, who came regularly to make tea. Jeanne will never forget one man. He just sat by himself, staring, not talking to anyone. She took him a mug of tea and asked if she could do anything to help. He told her he had helped to liberate Belsen. 'What we have seen I just can't tell you.'

After the war groups of Toc H members began once again to visit the birthplace of their movement. And with the launching of the programme of residential projects a new generation started to visit Poperinge. Sue Cumming, now a deacon in the Church of England, took part in a project there in 1966. They worked at de Lovie, a home for mentally handicapped young men about two miles out of Poperinge, and they tried also to learn something about life in Belgium, its history, its politics, its social system. While there they spent an evening with some Toc H members, veterans of the First World War. 'We were all in our teens or early twenties. We didn't really know much about the war, or about Toc H. In a sense we thought Toc H was formed to glorify the war. That was how we saw Remembrance Day, too.' So the first question was: why keep alive the memory of a war which had been such a terrible waste of men on both sides?

> We'd got our attack all lined up, but the wind was taken out of our sails completely by their answer to that first question, which was to the effect that Toc H came into being, not to glorify the war, but to remember what it had cost and in order that the spirit that was in those men in the trenches was handed on to people living together in a peacetime community. That was the way they could honour those men who had fallen, not by building memorials but by changing people's attitudes and by changing society. Well, of course we were thrown by this. They brought us to a new understanding of what the whole thing was about. I remember we had a service in the Upper Room later in the week and they asked us to contribute something. We sang, and got them singing, Bob Dylan's 'Blowing in the Wind'; and they felt as much for the words as we did. It all happened because we encountered one another, because we were in the same room, because we talked.

Those young people who visited Talbot House responded to its atmosphere. Peter Ranken first met Toc H at Talbot House when he was 16. As they drove home through Belgium after a family holiday his father remembered a Toc H Services' Club in Egypt that he'd known while doing his National Service ('one of the few places where you could meet Egyptians on equal terms') and decided to call at Talbot House. 'We only spent half an hour or so there', recalls Peter, 'but there was something about that building. It's difficult to explain. It has a specialness and also a certain strength within it; its history, what it meant to all the people who were involved.'

But, however great its impact on those who went there, it was difficult, in the 1960s and 1970s, to persuade people to go. Young people were engaged in, or at least sympathetic to, the widespread protests against the war in Vietnam and, like Sue Cumming, they saw the preservation of Talbot House as an attempt to glorify war. And they weren't much interested in history. They wanted to know where the movement was going, not where it had come from. By 1980 Talbot House was something of an embarrassment. Toc H couldn't just wash its hands of the building in which it had begun, yet only a handful of people visited the house and it cost a great deal to maintain.

And then suddenly the tide turned. There is a new interest in that period of history; and not just among Toc H members either. More and more people visit Flanders, and Toc H, to its surprise, finds itself with a tourist attraction on its hands. Over 10,000 people visited the house in 1988.

These visitors, especially those who stay for a few days, parties from schools and youth clubs as well as Toc H members, find that this old house doesn't only speak about the past; it speaks challengingly about the present and the future. As people attempt to understand the most terrible episode in the history of Europe, a story of courage and tenacity but also of futility and waste, they begin to realise how destructive are the conflicts in which all of us are caught up at one time or another, in our work, in our neighbourhoods, in our families.

A teacher took a group of pupils from his school to Talbot House and later showed slides of the visit at school assembly. At the end there wasn't the usual release of chatter and rush for the door. Everybody walked out quietly and thoughtfully. One of those who knew the house during the First World War called the chapel in the Upper Room 'a school of peace'. That could be said of the whole house today. In 1988 a Japanese woman, who now lives in Belgium, and whose grandmother was in Hiroshima when the atom bomb was dropped, gave the house a 'peace pole'. This simple white pole, with the words 'May Peace Prevail on Earth' in four languages, stands in the garden as a symbol of that continuing commitment.

11

Moving into Another World

Bill Bains and his friend Ray often used to talk together about people they knew who were in difficulties of one sort or another. It was 1958. Sunderland was a shipbuilding town subject to recurrent cycles of unemployment as the shipyards waited for the next order. They wanted to help in some way. One day Ray said he thought he'd found what they were looking for, and he showed Bill an article in *Reader's Digest* about the Revd 'Tubby' Clayton, the founder of Toc H. Toc H looked to Ray like an organisation through which their desire to help could be channelled, but Bill wasn't so sure. To him it looked like the kind of religious body in which he'd feel completely out of place.

Ray had been to half a dozen meetings of the Sunderland branch of Toc H before he could persuade Bill to go with him. Even then Bill went largely out of loyalty to Ray. He felt uncomfortable, not quite sure what was going on, but he was nonetheless impressed by the friendly, natural way in which he was made welcome. The branch at that time included a chemist, two probation officers, an accountant with the electricity board, the transport organiser for the local hospital and a solicitor's managing clerk. Bill was impressed by the way in which he, a crane driver, and Ray, a fitter, were accepted by these much older professional men.

They were not always very popular in the branch. They were inclined to embark on projects in the name of Toc H without the agreement, or sometimes even the knowledge, of their fellow-members. Not for them the delays and disappointments of working by persuasion. They did what they believed was right and hoped that some, at least, of their fellow-members would come with them.

Bill became a van driver with British Rail. His new job

meant that he took wheelchairs or artificial limbs to people with physical handicaps and he always made a point of having a chat with his customers. He discovered that there was a desperate need for a club for disabled people. He and Ray decided that the branch should call a public meeting and they persuaded the mayor to attend. The first meeting of the new club attracted only eight people but the Sunderland Society for the Disabled was born. In 1986, when the society celebrated its twenty-first birthday, there were more than a dozen clubs affiliated to it.

He and Ray were not content simply to maintain what they'd started. They were initiators by nature. They followed the launch of the Society for the Disabled by starting a club for handicapped children. The unique feature of this club was that, while the children played in one room, the parents had coffee in another. So the parents also had a social outlet and they were able to compare notes about equipment and where to find it.

Bill then arranged for the branch to visit Cherry Knowle Hospital to see whether there was anything they could do there. He had himself spent six months there when he was 18, following a mental breakdown. After coming out of hospital he had found it very difficult to get people to accept him. The stigma of mental illness remained. Talking to the Chief Mental Nurse he found that this was a common experience. About half the patients discharged were back in hospital within months because of this feeling of rejection. So Ray and Bill formed a club for ex-mental patients, something very similar to the friendship circles for which Toc H has become known more recently, though without the clearly articulated philosophy that circles have developed.

What attracted Bill to Toc H was not a philosophy; it was the opportunity to give practical help where it was needed. When the time came for the Ceremony of Light or prayers Bill would gather up the tea cups and go off to the kitchen to wash up. It was understood and accepted that he didn't attend prayers. No one tried to put pressure on him; but he himself became increasingly worried by his inability to play a full part in Toc H. Most of those he met in Toc H were Christians, the literature was quite explicitly Christian; and there was no way he could ever be part of that. He became deeply depressed. He felt he was letting Toc H down and letting other people down.

Secretly, every Saturday morning, he went to Bishop Wearmouth Church, where there was a small chapel that was always open. He sat at the back. He didn't kneel, or try to pray; he just sat, looking at the window or the altar. He would come out, after an hour or so, feeling a little better, but not much. One morning the curate came in and invited him to have a cup of tea. Bill didn't know what to do. Should he take the risk? After some moments of indecision he went through to the curate's house and a cup of tea with the curate, Philip, was added to Bill's Saturday morning routine.

Slowly, over several weeks, Philip persuaded Bill to make a list of all the things that were bothering him and then to make his Confession. When they got to that point Bill was none too happy but he didn't feel he could back out. He didn't want to disappoint Philip. Nonetheless he worried about it all week and by Saturday he was really upset. To make matters worse, Philip was caught in a traffic jam and kept him waiting.

They knelt down. Philip said a short prayer. Bill pulled the by now dog-eared list of worries from his pocket and read it out in a breathless gabble. Philip said another prayer and then he got up and said, 'What I'd like you to do now, Bill, is just to go home. We won't talk any more now.'

Bill left the church feeling very angry. He'd come for healing and he'd been fobbed off with a brief and meaningless piece of mumbo-jumbo. He barged his way through the people on the street; he just wanted to get away from the church as quickly as he could. And then, just as he was crossing Wearmouth Bridge, his anger suddenly left him. He could hardly stop himself from laughing aloud. And then, seconds later, he had a feeling of deep peace such as he had never experienced before. It was like being in another world altogether. Now, more than 20 years later, that extraordinary sense of peace is still vivid in his memory. His life has had many ups and downs since then. He still has times of self-hatred. But through it all he has been upheld and sustained by that one profound experience.

One of the places to which Bill's delivery runs took him was Washington, about to become a major New Town. The three pits had closed. A new population of 30–40,000 was to be added to the present 17,000 people, who lived in three distinct villages. As Bill made his rounds and chatted with people, in their homes or in the shops, he became aware how worried everyone was about what was going to happen; and he thought that Toc H ought to be doing something to bring the existing population and the newcomers together.

He talked to the area committee of Toc H, of which he was now a member. He told them about the people's worries – strangers would be coming from all over the country; their houses would be pulled down; they would be moved to a different place. He spoke about the challenge, and the opportunity, which this represented. 'You'd better do something about it then', was the response.

So he did. He knew a bit about clubs for handicapped people and he knew, through his deliveries of artificial limbs and other aids, a number of handicapped people in Washington. The membership of the Washington Society for the Disabled, which he formed, was drawn from the established population and from the newcomers and its first secretary was a young woman paralysed from the waist down.

Meanwhile Bill lost his job, as part of the British Rail cutbacks initiated by Dr Beeching. The manager of the Labour Exchange, knowing something of his work with Toc H, recommended that he should train as a social worker. Bill's immediate reaction was that he was 'quite mad'. He was 37. He'd left school at 14. With a wife and four children he obviously couldn't afford to go on a course. But his friends in Toc H encouraged him to apply to Ruskin College. 'I wasn't very keen, to be absolutely honest, but people were being so kind I just felt I had to go on the course.' Anonymous contributions from Toc H members and grants from charitable trusts made it just possible for him to spend two years in Oxford. The greatest contribution of all was made by his wife Jean, who took a job as a cleaner at a Salvation Army hostel. 'She had to clear up after alcoholics, sick all over the place. She did that for two years, and looked after four children.'

Oxford for Bill was a magical experience, 'almost like being cocooned. My mind would go back to all the books I'd read, like *Tom Brown's Schooldays*. I'd become part of the public school system.' But for Jean those two years were very different. Not only the hard work but the feeling that Bill was, in some ways, drifting away from her. One half-term, when he had a psychology essay to write, he brought some of the books home. Coming back from the pub one night he found Jean reading one of the books. 'I've got to know something,' she said, 'else I'll not be able to talk to you.' 'We don't relate at an intellectual level,' says Bill, 'it's at a "Bill and Jean" level that we relate. Which is best.' The reading he does, the TV programmes he watches, the people who visit him, all set Bill apart from Jean and from the children. 'There's a difference between "dad" and the job. I've tried to diminish it in their eyes but I've never been able to achieve it.'

After completing the course at Ruskin Bill returned to Toc H, as a member of the full-time staff. Becoming an employee of Toc H meant a physical move from Sunderland to Leeds but mentally he'd already moved away from his roots. When he came home from college and went to the pub he felt people no longer talked to him as they used to. 'I said to Ray: "What's wrong?"and Ray said: "You're a clever dick. You've left them behind. You know it all now." I used to think the same way before. People from a different strata of society, or with a better education, were a different kind of animal.' He'd joined the middle class. 'It's almost like becoming a traitor. You feel you've reneged on some kind of loyalty or another. It's a strange phenomenon.'

In the eyes of his old friends his job with Toc H wasn't a 'real' job. He wasn't doing any physical labour. It was an effeminate way of life. And there was a part of Bill that didn't see it as a real job either. He felt guilty if he wasn't on the move all the time. He felt tremendous pressure to produce, to show what he could do, and he spent much of his first three years driving all over Yorkshire. Looking back he thinks 'it was all a bit of an ego trip'.

Bill's life journey has changed him fundamentally. He has, painfully, crossed the class divide; and he has, equally painfully, come to terms with his ingrained suspicion of all things religious. But in many ways he remains the same. He's still an activist and an initiator, seeing it as his job, as a member of the Toc H staff, to pioneer new forms of service. And he still holds on to that single 'mystical' experience on Wearmouth

Bridge. 'Before that I was doing things but they didn't seem to have any meaning or purpose. That element was missing. Until I had that experience I wasn't happy with myself. I count on that. When I get really down I remember it. Since then I seem to have been channelled in some way.'

12

Planting Seeds

Mick Tierney was a corporal in the Army Medical Corps, stationed at Paderborn in West Germany, when he first met Toc H. He was asked to look after a group of young volunteers who were coming to run a play scheme for army children, and he wasn't best pleased. They'd all be students and he didn't think much of students, 'all going round with dreams in their heads, save the whale and all that stuff. A bunch of wallies, that's what I thought of 'em.'

It was Mick's job to act as the link between the army, which provided equipment and transport, and the volunteers. He recruited a friend to help him and to act as minibus driver. 'Me and me mate decided we'd take them at face value. If they were alright with us, we'd be alright with them.' When they got to the airport they found just what they'd expected – 'you know, students, teachers, that sort of thing, nice, middle-class people'. But as they drove to Paderborn they found something else which they hadn't expected. These people were friendly and interested. They seemed keen to learn about life in the army. And they invited Mick and his friend the driver to take part in the play scheme, and to share in running activities for the children.

Running activities for children was no problem to Mick, who'd done plenty of youth work in his time. But the play scheme offered him something more. He was forced to spend three weeks with people who were totally different, and in the process he discovered that these middle-class students weren't the 'wallies' he'd assumed them to be. 'I found it fascinating talking about things. They talked about their sort of life, which was alien to me. I'd be showing them my sort of life which was alien to them. It was just amazing to find out about different backgrounds, different things. Like violence.

To them it was terrible but to me it was a way of life. If you had an argument you had a fight and that was it.'

Not that either the volunteers or Mick himself found mixing easy. The volunteers spent a lot of time talking about 'exams and such'. They used words Mick didn't know and discussed concepts he didn't understand. And when Mick took the volunteers to soldiers' bars they were equally out of their depth. On the first occasion Tim, the male leader of the group, started dancing to the music. A soldier grabbed a chair, and put it in the middle of the room. He told Tim to stand on it, gave him a pint of beer and said he must down it in eight seconds. 'Fair play to 'im – it must've been quite frightening for 'im – he done it. And at the end he put the beer pot on 'is 'ead. And as soon as he done that he was accepted. Even if he'd tried it and failed it wouldn't have mattered. He broke the ice by doing that. It was a little challenge. But he done it. That really helped.'

Through all these new experiences, deep friendships developed, of a kind which Mick had never experienced before. 'I had a lot of mates in the army but not like that. It was like a family.' When the volunteers returned home Mick felt that there was a great hole in his life. And he was surprised to find that he wanted to keep in touch with these people – 'which again in the army you just didn't do. We still bloody argue. We don't agree. But there's still that friendship there.'

These play schemes in Germany are part of the programme of short-term residential projects launched in the 1960s. When people are living together the timescale is telescoped and the experience is intensified. When they are also engaged together in some demanding piece of work the process speeds up even further. 'The most powerful experiences I've had with Toc H', says staff member Philip Douch, 'have all been residential; and that's where I've seen other people growing the most.'

Toc H began in a house in Flanders. After the war it was reborn in a house; and Toc H houses (marks as they were called) were established during the 1920s and 1930s in many of the major cities of England. Since the 1960s Toc H has also offered residential experiences through projects and at conference and training centres. The original marks have gradually been replaced by smaller community houses. Accommodation that was acceptable in the 1930s no longer met the demands of young people in the 1970s. Upstairs there were iron bedsteads and brown lino, reminiscent of an old-fashioned boarding school. Downstairs were battered leather armchairs, like a gentleman's club that had fallen on hard times.

Ken Butterfield, now a social worker with deaf people, lived in four different Toc H houses during that period of transition. He was the honorary warden of the mark in Leicester in the early 1970s, and he recalls how difficult it was to keep the mark full. 'Not everybody wanted to live in a Toc H mark. Our biggest room held six residents. People were beginning to feel, it's a nice place, good food, lovely atmosphere and all the rest of it, but I don't really want to share with five other chaps.'

It was while living in the Leicester mark, however, that he decided that his future lay, not as he had imagined in insurance broking, but in social work. He moved to Birmingham and found that the mark there was very different. It was another large, rambling building but it had only 16 residents, all in single rooms. No meals were provided, residents cooked for themselves. And the building was not just a residence, it was a centre for Toc H projects. Jennifer Mitchell, who ran the house with her husband John, later to become Director of Toc H, recalls a 'soup run' to people sleeping rough in the city, 'a little, little beginning which grew'. Those first tentative beginnings were to lead eventually to the establishment of the Trinity Centre for homeless men, with which several Toc H members are still active.

A project in Hampshire, running activities for travellers' children, was followed by a visit to Birmingham by some of the children. 'I mean, what travellers from anywhere in the country', says Jennifer, 'would allow their children to go on holiday with people elsewhere? And yet they came. That sort of thing was just staggering.'

Ken Butterfield's particular interest was the Toc H Birmingham Outward Group, whose voluntary leaders took young people, many of whom had been in trouble with the law, on adventure weekends, rock-climbing, fell-walking, canoeing. 'I enjoy being with young people and I enjoy the outdoor life. Going out on the hills with the Outward Group combined both these things. A lot of it is about getting people you help to help others, having young deaf people come on weekends, teaching them to use a compass, giving them responsibilities and then having them come to you saying: "Look, I feel confident enough to take a group to the Lakes. What d'you think?" '

In 1959 Toc H obtained a centre where people could come together for projects and conferences, an old stone house in the Cotswolds called Dor Knap. It wasn't grand in any way, more like an extended cottage, but it had a kind of magic. People grow misty-eyed when they talk about it. 'My first memory', says Sue Cumming, 'is of it being very cold, so that we had to sit on one another's knees to keep warm, and light a fire in the inglenook fireplace, and the smoke came down the chimney rather than going up, so the room was full of woodsmoke.'

Since the lease of Dor Knap expired Toc H has had other centres, some for conferences, others as bases for outdoor activities, like the house in the Lake District used for many of the Outward Group weekends, but none has been quite so special. The latest Toc H centre, however, Lindridge House in Devon, acquired in 1985, is already developing a magic of its own.

It was conceived primarily as a place where projects would take place. Philip Douch, who runs Lindridge with his wife, Jane, wanted to 'be sure of offering to anybody who was new to Toc H an experience which would be likely to be a true expression of what the movement's about and also would be likely to lead to further involvement. The surest way of doing that seemed to me, still seems to me, to be a short, one-off, no-strings-attached, residential commitment. If they want more, great; but they don't sign up for a weekend on the understanding that they're committing their lives for the next six months. Some may subsequently commit themselves quite heavily in a variety of ways, but variety of ways is the key phrase. There's a whole range of stuff. There's almost certainly something, somewhere, that they would find it easy and comfortable to slip into. And it's all come about much more easily by virtue of having a place.'

Philip and Jane Douch have great natural charm, an ease of manner that is immediately attractive to people of all ages. It would be very easy to put the undoubted success of

Lindridge House down simply to that and to overlook the professionalism with which they have approached the job. It shows in quite small ways, like the welcome people receive when they first arrive. 'That's a first and major step towards getting everything else right', says Philip. 'We try to ensure that people don't get to the front door before we do, so that people are met before they have to decide which of the two doors to knock on. It's not difficult but it's very easy to overlook.'

Lindridge House has developed an expertise in its own particular kind of small group work which is widely recognised in the area. Groups of six children with special needs come regularly to stay with an equal number of volunteers on a one-to-one basis. 'I think it's surprising', says Annette Jones, the social worker responsible, 'what people can cope with in a small group environment. It seems to stretch the children without there being too much difference from home.' Dave Weinstock, who works at a home for adults with learning difficulties, echoes her words: 'It was a creative weekend – they had to do things, find things, be stretched. They found themselves living with other people on equal terms.' It's this opportunity to work on a one-to-one basis which attracts many of the volunteers. 'I come with Toc H', says one, 'because I know I'll get close to the other people, whether "clients" or volunteers.'

Lindridge House, like the project programme itself, was designed to attract *young people* to Toc H. Both have in fact attracted a much wider age range. Pen Bayley was in her forties and recently divorced when she went on her first project. She was 'terrified' beforehand, convinced that she'd be quite unable to cope with handicapped children. 'I could never have believed I could have had such a good time when I expected it to be so terrible. It absolutely staggered me.' Nor did she find a problem in mixing with volunteers who were much younger than herself. 'That's the thing I've found in Toc H. You're just who you are. They don't seem to label people – at least that's been my experience so far.'

Liz Jones, now a bookshop manager in Birmingham, was just 17 when she went on her first project. It was a similarly euphoric experience. 'It was so different to anything I'd done before. It was my first time away from home, my first time of living with a group of people who had, to some degree, different experiences of life. The weather was glorious, the leader was loopy – I'd never met anyone so loopy before. Everything happened in a very easy way, so much so that we lost all track of time, like being in a little idyllic world. It's one of those things that's very intangible, very unquantifiable, so that when I got home it was very difficult to describe it. I wanted to understand why that experience had meant so much, what was behind it, how it was such a powerful thing.'

But, of course, there's a danger that projects may become, in Philip Douch's words, 'a one-off, unreal "high"'. It's essential that people are continually challenged and stretched. Liz Jones says that her second project, decorating for old people in Birmingham, was 'much more of an eye-opener, putting me in situations which I'd never experienced, meeting people who'd obviously had a very tough life'. And Peter Ranken recalls that 'the most amazing thing of that week was right at the end when the two leaders said: "We think you could lead one of these things." I nearly fell over. I was 17. Me look after two minibuses, a dozen volunteers and everything else? I thought this was just crazy.' A few months later he was invited to a leaders' weekend and, in the same letter, he was informed which project he would be leading and who his co-leader would be. 'So I was somewhat bounced into it.' He has led Toc H projects more or less every year since then but he doubts whether he would ever have got started if he hadn't been 'bounced into it' at the beginning.

If projects are to stretch people they must have a real mixture and that isn't easy. As the programme grows – there were 62 in the summer months of 1989 – it also extends throughout the year and includes many more weekends; and just occasionally a quite remarkable variety of people are brought together. In the autumn of 1989 one project group consisted of: two young men on probation (one of whom has been invited to lead future projects); one 50-year-old Toc H member; the manager of a Birmingham AIDS hostel; two 16-year-old Asian girls; one disabled woman who works as a clerical assistant; and two British Rail employees, one a manager and one a guard (and there was a rail strike at the time).

The challenge to individuals may well, at some point, be to seek new experiences outside Toc H. Liz Jones is grateful that she had 'that contact, and that intensity of contact. It gave me an immense amount. I was challenged to think about my priorities in life, the things that mattered to me, and all in a very loving, supportive atmosphere.' But eventually she felt she had to cut her links with Toc H completely. She had 'got too submerged in it. I actually believed very strongly that I would find it very difficult to function outside the world of Toc H. That's the extent to which I drowned in it.'

Ken Butterfield feels 'guilty' about not doing more for 'an organisation that's given me so much'. Yet he has started an Outward Group in Clwyd modelled precisely on the Toc H Outward Group in Birmingham; and he says that what he is doing at the outdoor activities centre for deaf children and adults, which he runs with his wife Janet, 'is due in no small measure to the experiences that I had with Toc H'.

If projects are to have this kind of lasting impact there must be an atmosphere which encourages people to reflect. 'The only compulsory part I would want to impose on a project', says Philip Douch, 'is that people *must* talk about what's happened at the end of the day. It's important to look at what went on, how it could be improved, and what does improving it mean. That might not be particularly profound but it's signalling that looking at what we're doing is as important as doing it.'

And so at Lindridge House there's a quiet room, a place where people can go apart and reflect. It's in the heart of the house and yet feels separate. There's a carpet on the floor and cushions, as well as chairs, to sit on. There's a wide selection of books which people may find helpful but there are no religious symbols on the walls; it's not a chapel. 'The hope is', says Philip, 'that everyone will be able to find what they can, and take what they will, by being quiet and reflective. It's been used in different ways by different groups, and on different terms by different individuals.' The simple fact that it's there is in itself a public demonstration that Toc H regards reflection as an important part of any activity. 'It's a powerful signal to people. In many ways that's its most important function, to plant seeds in people's minds.'

The whole atmosphere of a project leads people to think, perhaps for the first time, about what's important to them in life, though it's sometimes difficult for them to find the language in which to express their thoughts and feelings. One volunteer put it this way: 'When people in a group are working and having a laugh together, especially in a high-pressured residential situation like a project, I'm sure that this is the way people ought to live together – not because it's morally correct or anything stuffy like that, but because it just feels so right.'

13

Significance

In the ambulants' ward the staff were simply trying to make sure that the patients didn't hurt each other. It was a rainy day and everyone was indoors. A small boy with a crash helmet was knocking his head repeatedly against a wall. Sue Cumming was 18 and had no experience with children suffering from severe mental handicap. 'I sat down on a bench next to a little boy who was just rocking himself backwards and forwards. It turned out that he was nine years old but he had the mentality of a six-month-old baby.' She didn't know what to do. She said 'Hallo': he looked at her and then away. Talking produced no response so after half an hour she tried tickling him: 'and at that point he smiled. It was an amazing breakthrough for me . . . there was a real encounter.'

This was only the beginning:

> During that week I discovered an amazing and unexpected joy working with those children and also among the group of volunteers. We laughed and laughed and laughed. We *played* together. It brought the child out of us all. We also discussed together – well, what about euthanasia, what about children who are born already so badly deformed, surely it's kinder to kill them? Being able to say the unforgiveable and then decide that no, that wasn't the answer, these were precious human beings, who mattered as much to God as anyone else. And I saw that the parents who came were devastated by what had happened and so many were *laden* with guilt. I found in myself – again, quite unexpectedly – a spontaneous compassion. And for the first time I understood what compassion meant and I thought gosh, this is what's spoken of in the Gospels. Because until then it had been I *ought* to do this, I *ought* to help, which

> came from my Methodist upbringing. And suddenly finding it was a natural response as well as a moral response was a joyful discovery.

Sue was born in 1947, 'part of the postwar baby bulge'. Like Julia Lane, who is a few years younger, she is highly educated and articulate, from a middle-class background in which 'the social gospel' was an integral part of daily life. Both had *new* experiences through Toc H; but both describe its effect on their lives as one, above all, of illumination. It showed them the significance of what they were already doing and of what they had always believed.

Julia went on her first holiday with the mentally handicapped when she was at Cambridge and enjoyed it so much that she went every year for about eight years. One year she couldn't find one to go on until she came across a Toc H projects booklet. It was an enjoyable holiday, but no different from any other that she'd been on – until the last night, when a member of staff who happened to be there as a volunteer started getting people to talk about what they'd got out of the fortnight: 'He drew it out gently, so you didn't realise what was happening until afterwards; just trying to move it onto a higher plane. I was absolutely bowled over because I realised I hadn't really noticed it all before. Yes, there'd been a fellowship and everything on *all* the holidays but I'd just taken it for granted . . .' For her, this *awareness* is what is so special about all Toc H encounters; she defines it as an acknowledgement that 'there is a spiritual dimension' – which is not the same as religious belief:

> It's a kind of denial of self. You're giving up a Saturday afternoon because you believe that you're not the only person on this earth and you're doing it with Toc H because it isn't just about the physically disabled or people with leprosy or whatever . . . The very diversity of it means that it's people who have a principle in mind. They don't have a particular mission to help one section of society, which is what I started off with. I could have gone on like that for a long time but in fact I ended up painting walls, working with the disabled, gardening, nursing . . . It's important that there are people in Toc H who don't believe in God but who are still prepared to do the same things.

> I'd rather use the word 'spiritual' than 'religious' – in a secular kind of way.

She had been brought up in South West Lancashire in the 1950s in 'a real Catholic ghetto', not meeting anyone who wasn't a Catholic until she was at least 16. 'Because of that one lived out one's faith during the week as well as on Sundays. I've never found it to be the same in any community I've lived in since.' The women in particular were deeply involved in voluntary work as their children grew up. It didn't occur to them to go out to work, which would have been 'undignified'. But it wasn't just the women who were active in this way – everybody did something and at school it was even part of the curriculum. The fabric of Catholic ritual enfolded their lives: before they went on holiday they checked out the times of Mass at the local church, and fish on Fridays was a must, whatever the boarding house menu.

It is a way of life which has largely disappeared now. Julia has witnessed the disillusionment and even loss of faith of many people she knew, who were irredeemably confused by the reforms of the Church's Second Vatican Council in the early 1960s. She is the only one of her own family who has retained her faith. Although she has 'lapsed' in the past she is now intellectually as well as emotionally committed to Catholicism – but she has moved a long way from her upbringing. She is married to an Anglican of an evangelical inclination and feels that she has been enormously enriched by this. Their shared Christian faith is very important to them, and they have reached compromises about the baptism and upbringing of children and so on. Discussion and prayer have replaced regulations: 'You can't have an absolute set of values and a conscience as well . . . people nowadays make all their own decisions. God is God, but religion is a man-made thing.'

The 'unconditional love' which Julia found in Toc H, and which she had previously come across only in the mentally handicapped, was one of the things which changed her. Crippled by shyness, she was given confidence by the natural warmth of the 'wonderful hotchpotch' of people at the London branch she became involved in. At one point she was giving over almost every evening to committees and an endless stream of activities, despite the long and demanding hours of her job. Her own timidity was intimately bound up with her tendency to stereotype others. One individual whom she met when they were painting a hostel for battered wives, did more than anybody else to break down her fears – although she doesn't know his name and can't even remember what he looked like:

> I started painting this long wall and this young boy started after me at the other end. So we were moving towards one another. And as we got within conversational distance I started to panic because I'd heard him speaking about his probation officer and I thought 'Well, I'm a lawyer working with a City firm of solicitors – what's he going to think of me?' . . . I couldn't cope with other people's reactions to me . . . We got to the middle of the wall and for some strange reason that was the first thing he asked me – what I did. And it clearly didn't matter to him a bit! We just chatted and I just felt all this relief draining out of me.

She was puzzled as to why someone with a probation officer should be on a weekend like that:

> It was a very significant moment and he was a very significant person, because I thought – he may have a probation officer and he may have committed a crime but that's got nothing to do with it. He's a person who wants to do something for other people and wants to be with us. It altered my way of looking at other people, because where I'd put people in categories, I realised you didn't need to do that. Particularly with Toc H, because there was a method, a means of expressing yourself.

Julia's Catholicism has always caused her to feel slightly distanced from Toc H, which 'sometimes feels like a branch of Anglicanism'. She kept the different parts of her life separate. For Sue Cumming, however, Toc H was a longed for spiritual home. On one of her first weekend projects, at Easter in the year she left school, she realised that she had discovered a group of people 'whom deep down I knew I'd been longing to meet but didn't dare believe existed'. The first thing to impress her was that every issue was open for discussion and she was particularly astonished when the chaplain led a debate on the nature of God: 'I'd never come across a minister who talked like that.' It was also permissible to poke fun at anything and everything – even religion: 'We had one lad who was very ticklish and one day we tickled him to death and then went and picked a daffodil from outside and held a mock funeral.' At this point the chaplain appeared: 'I was expecting him to say "stop being silly"; but he *joined in.* He just said some very solemn words – and of course we were absolutely hysterical.'

There was a warmth of fellowship and a genuine care which overwhelmed her; and it was on this weekend that she first came face to face with someone who'd been to a public school – and found that he was not a 'toffee-nosed kid' but an individual with a concern for the slums of Liverpool. It was not only encounters with people which took her aback. The communion service on Easter Sunday was the first one she'd ever attended where wine rather than grape juice was used: 'I remember the sensation as this alcoholic wine hit the back of my throat. It was an amazing spiritual experience because I suddenly thought – yes, this isn't cloying and sweet. This is sharp – this is the blood of Christ.'

It was experiences such as these which kept her within the Christian Church; but the most critical spiritual and personal turning point in her life took her away from direct involvement with Toc H. While she was on the staff in Nottingham in the late 1970s, and finding the job increasingly lonely and difficult, she became closely connected with the University chaplaincy. She noticed that it was when her conversations with young people turned to their exploration of faith, that she felt she was 'doing something really important'. At the same time she became aware that the Methodist Church had started to ordain women. The first service she attended taken by a woman impressed her as being very good – and markedly different from any other she had ever been to. Aware of a growing desire to be somehow trained to utilise better the skills she knew she had, she began, rather nervously, to wonder if she had a vocation to the ministry. But she had no desire to go away from Nottingham, where she had begun to put down roots – and there seemed no way that she could stay if she did indeed have a calling. 'I began to feel almost like a piece of paper being sort of torn into pieces and tossed away . . . a terrible feeling of psychological disintegration.'

Then she discovered an Anglican, non-residential training course based at Nottingham University and enrolled. Shortly after she started she 'had this sensation one day of being drawn along a corridor, and it had no features at all. It was sort of a dim corridor – it was dark and there wasn't any bright light or anything. I had this sensation of being moved along it – I wasn't making any effort. But I couldn't see where it was leading.' Half way through the course she found herself thinking that if she were an Anglican she would like to become a deaconess. At this point 'it was as if I'd turned a *slight* corner, an imperceptible bend in the corridor; and at the very far end there was a tiny chink of light shining through'.

She was confirmed as an Anglican and became a deaconess in 1982. In 1984 she married one of her tutors. The work she has done since, both in a parish and now as Diocesan Adviser in Parish Education, has made good use of her teaching as well as her theological qualifications. Her Toc H experience has also been invaluable, above all for the assumptions it had sown in her about the futility of hierarchy and the potential closeness in professional relationships. On a diocesan residential weekend she was struck by how edgy and guarded people were: 'the kind of warmth and ease of approach that we reached at the end of the weekend was where Toc H weekends started!'

She feels enormously privileged to be a participant in 'a *fascinating* transition period'. She remembers with amusement how in the early seventies a number of the male members of the Toc H staff had had no idea how to deal with their female colleagues – and how some of the clergymen had been the worst of all. She knows too that she unknowingly colluded with sexism in the guise of flattery or flirtation. Now she is far more aware, but no more strident in her feminism than she was then. She remembers the jolt she received when she first saw a woman's name in the 'preacher' slot on a Methodist notice board and knows that simply by being in certain places as an ordained woman and by taking on certain roles, she is breaking down barriers.

Sue Cumming and Julia Lane are women who have taken it for granted that education, marriage and a career were as much their right as any man's. Their lives have been largely shaped by the religious upbringing they received in tight-knit, convinced, faith communities. But for both of them it was Toc H which put flesh on the bones of belief. When Sue first realised that her sense of compassion was spontaneous rather than dutiful, she connected her feelings for the first time with 'that other part that had been labelled faith but was in fact learned doctrine, and it was the point at which that came to life'. Julia had always been aware of a dimension other than the purely material in her own life and in that of other 'religious' people; but through Toc H she saw that her definition of spirituality was too narrow. 'It changed my attitude to other people – I realise now that there is potential and . . . *significance* . . . in everybody.'

14

More Questions than Answers

Peter Ranken lives in a cluttered flat in Leytonstone, East London. He's an architect and as you look round the walls your eye is drawn to elevations of some of the great buildings of the Italian Renaissance. He talks for the most part with thoughtful deliberation but every now and then he speeds up, either from shyness or enthusiasm, compressing whole phrases into single syllables. Only as you think back over the conversation do you realise that, in his own tentative way, he has uncovered some of the far-reaching issues facing Toc H today.

After his first experience of projects he was invited to work full time for Toc H for nine months, in return for board and lodging and pocket money. 'That was brilliant, one of the best times ever.' It was a time when he 'learned quite a lot about myself, what I can do and what I can't do'. Above all, it offered the experience of being challenged by two colleagues, the Revd Bob Knight and John Dickson, to 'think about my understanding of what Toc H meant, especially the spiritual and religious side. Working with Bob, somebody who's done a lot of thinking about that, and to whom it's very important to get people, especially young people, to think about their religious experiences, was a wonderful thing. That was great, to have someone you could speak to as an equal, even though, in terms of age and everything else, he was very different.'

Peter had had only limited exposure to religion before joining Toc H but 'various things happened during that year which caused me to think about it a lot more'. He remembers a conference weekend when there was a religious service, which everyone had to attend, in a very traditional form.

I thought, this is not my understanding of what this is all about. I gulped and sat down and refused to take part in the rest of the service. I was livid afterwards. How dare someone impose something on me which didn't fit! Which forced me to think about the sort of things that do fit, to work things out for myself – which I'm still in the process of doing.

The only things which really make sense are those which are grounded in your own experience. A few days ago at work people were saying they'd never had a religious experience and stuff like that. I didn't say anything because I had other things to do but I would have disputed that. There are certain things. They mean something and they make sense and you decide to put words to them; or you don't decide to put words to them, just reckon they were something special. It can be difficult if you're not from a particular religious background to realise you don't have to be put off by the various words, that not all of them mean you'll be a hypocrite if you believe in them. That nine months with Toc H caused me to think about that a lot more and in bursts I will do some reading, and I will speak to people about it, and will try to progress my thoughts in that department, the inner life or whatever – to use one of the phrases I still have problems with. That's what it is, but then . . . But it doesn't jar as much as some other phrases.

Peter has more questions than answers. He has difficulty finding the words to convey his experience and the conclusions which he draws from it; but he is convinced about the importance of continuing to search for meaning. 'You have to try to be aware of what happens to you.' And there are things which can only be explained in a religious way, which seem 'to fit in with your concept of – I'm not sure how to phrase this – the spiritual side, of a living presence, or a loving being – in fact it's very much tied up with that. The good things are connected with love, and there's something religious to that. It's very easy to ignore that. There are times when you spend weeks and months and years not thinking about it, or only occasionally thinking about it, and then something will happen – and bang, this is actually what it's all about.'

For Peter, one of those deeply significant experiences happened in South Africa. When he heard that Toc H was recruiting a small group of volunteers to work with Toc H South Africa during the summer of 1985 he was immediately interested but he finally made up his mind to apply only days before the deadline. He was concerned that by going to South Africa he 'would be supporting what was going on there'. On the other hand 'to visit another country and actually do something there is always a better way of getting to know the place'. He was attracted by the opportunity of visiting 'a country which is so much a focus of negative world opinion, and to go and see it with an organisation that was in a position to give a reasonable view of most sections of that society'. At the same time he wanted to get back to Africa, where he had lived for a few years during his childhood. 'I realised I have quite a strong emotional connection with that continent.' And, after several years of leading projects, he was looking for a new challenge, a new way 'to test myself, to put myself on the line. That's what Toc H is about, giving people challenges.'

The first few days in South Africa he was 'absorbing everything, like a sponge, and being reminded of so many things, the heat, the dryness, everything else'. The six British volunteers spent three weeks at the newly established Toc H centre at Carletonville, a few miles from Johannesburg, in the brown, beige and yellow of the barren veldt. Accommodation was in huts on a 30-acre site made available by the Anglo-American Corporation, close to the shaft of the world's deepest gold mine. Each week they were joined by South African volunteers, from different racial groups and different parts of the country. Part of the time was spent running activities for visiting groups of children or disabled people, the rest in physical work on the site.

The powerful experience, whose full meaning Peter is still trying to uncover, occurred during the third week. A group of children from Soweto, the huge black township near Johannesburg, came to the centre for the day. It was Peter's turn to be leader of the volunteer group that week and he arranged a conventional morning of games and crafts. During the lunch break one of the girls from Soweto asked if she could 'do a turn' and he naturally agreed. He assumed that this would take five, or at the most ten, minutes and then they would carry on with the treasure hunt arranged for the afternoon. 'In fact this "turn" involved everybody, blacks, whites, everybody who was there, and it lasted an hour and a half. We were all singing and dancing and playing games, organised by the children. We didn't understand what was going on half the time. That was the fun of it. They were singing in Zulu and Tswana and Xhosa.' The magic of that hour and a half is still vividly alive for him as he talks.

Partly the magic lay in the discovery that these children, whose lives were so poor and so constricted, could plan and organise something as complex as this, and had the cohesion to carry it through without any disagreements or arguments. 'People just said "16" or whatever and the game changed.'

At a more personal level the magic lay in recognising that he, as the appointed and accepted leader, had simply to let go, to allow it to happen. 'As an approach to life, making sense of life and these magic moments, this means a lot. Let go, don't worry about it too much, just let it happen. It's very difficult to do.'

And then again the children were saying, to someone who was older, someone who was white, 'We too have something precious to give'; and showing that they trusted these white volunteers enough to offer it.

> They were saying, 'You're friendly enough, you're batty enough, you're open, not like a lot of the whites we come across, therefore we feel happy to do this.' It was a great privilege for us. I began to realise how different society could be, in South Africa and in lots of countries in the world, if that sort of attitude could prevail more often. You can't engineer it, only do your best to provide the environment where that can happen. That's what we did on that day, outside Johannesburg, near a mine, where it wasn't black land, it wasn't white land, it was in the middle of nowhere. It was just brilliant. It was a clue to how life might be lived. I'm still coming to terms with it.

After the three weeks at the Toc H centre in Carletonville the British volunteers visited Toc H groups in white suburbs and in black townships. They spent a day at the notorious Crossroads squatter camp outside Cape Town, which brought home to them 'how awful the situation is in that country'. When they returned home Peter was asked to lead the group that would go to South Africa the following year. He found the atmosphere on that second trip quite different, largely, he feels, because of the changing political situation.

When the first trip was planned there seemed to be 'a window of opportunity where Toc H could actually do something' by bringing black and white together. But that summer violence broke out and a State of Emergency was declared. 'We saw Botha declaring it on TV, which is a very chilling thing to see. It's a powerful thing, to be watching it in a comfortable white suburb, and to know that things are happening all around you, bonfires are erupting, and yet it doesn't physically affect you.'

By 1986, then, there was 'a crisis of confidence among white Toc H in South Africa. A lot of people involved with Toc H in South Africa are very well-meaning people but they are not especially political. Sometimes that means they do very good work, because they don't worry about that. At other times it means they are incredibly patronising, unbelievably so. A lot of them were not quite sure where they stood, aware that they could have some of their liberties taken away if they were as radical as it could be argued they should be, in view of what Toc H stands for.'

Peter's visits to South Africa have developed within him a political awareness, a recognition that the kind of values which give meaning to his life can't be divorced from politics. Toc H from the beginning has tried to bring together people with differing viewpoints in an attempt to create peace instead of conflict. It has set out to attract people of all political persuasions and therefore it has never acted as a political pressure group, preferring to try to change people's attitudes at an individual, personal level. 'I do not wish', wrote Peter Monie, the first Administrator of Toc H, in *Toc H Under Weigh*, published in 1927, 'to wake up in the morning and find Toc H developed into a propagandist society, even if I entirely agree with the cause it proposes to support.' He went on to argue that Toc H is of its essence an inclusive fellowship, something that can be called, and not in any superficial or sentimental sense, a 'family'. We cannot risk breaking up the family, however noble the cause or however small the minority who have to leave because they cannot support it. The argument is persuasive, and has been generally accepted within Toc H over the years; but, as Peter Ranken learned in South Africa, there are nonetheless situations where 'you have to take sides, because if you don't you will be seen to have taken the side of the people who are imposing the *status quo*'.

Toc H talks about bringing people together, about reconciliation, about defusing situations, but that can be 'like taking the fuses out but the bombs are still there; you're not getting rid of them'. For any real reconciliation to take place there has to be 'honest respect on both sides and a willingness to give on both sides'. The meeting of people from different classes, different races, can simply be an attempt to make the *status quo* more palatable; or it can be an open, honest encounter between people who are willing to have their opinions and attitudes challenged, and possibly changed. 'You have to know when you're being honest with yourself, and when you're not. It's easy to delude yourself into thinking you're being honest.'

Over the past year Peter has been 'drifting away' from Toc H. There's an element of disillusion and staleness about this but there's also something very much more positive. 'I'm thinking seriously, after gaining sufficient experience in this country, that I will work abroad, being paid at local rates, doing social architecture. Yet recognising also (this is one of the things I learnt from going to South Africa) that much as I'm emotionally linked to Africa, I'm still English. England is still my home.' There's much in the experiences and challenges which he has enjoyed through Toc H which is as yet unresolved in his mind.

> I've reached the stage where I need to reflect on what's happened. A lot of the things that have caused me to think about religion – no, the spiritual life rather than religion, because religion has various other connotations – have been while I was doing Toc H things. Not all of them, but a lot. I've reached the stage when I need to reflect on that. Reflection can take place soon after a particular event,

equally it can take place over a long period of time. I think my understanding of what happened on the two trips to South Africa is still going on and still needs to be sorted out.

For Peter, Toc H has been a succession of challenges, challenges to try new things, to test his abilities in new ways. And, at a deeper and more fundamental level, it has been a constant challenge to explore the mystery of life and the meaning of human relationships. 'It's important that that should still be there in whatever Toc H does in the future.' It's very easy, when there's a lot of activity going on, for that most important challenge of all to be forgotten or evaded. 'People with a particular religious and spiritual background and training need to be around to challenge people at various points.'

As people respond to the challenge they will begin to find a language which will, for them, express the meaning of their own experiences. 'On good projects a group will develop its own language to explain certain things that meant a lot to it.' Whether that language means anything to people outside the group doesn't really matter. What does matter is the sharing of understanding within the group. The Revd Bob Knight often used to say to Peter, during the year when they worked together: 'If you know where one person stands, and you know where somebody else stands, you've got two bearings from which you can try to work out where you stand yourself.'

15

'Such a Lot of Wisdom'

In a filing cabinet drawer in the Social Work Department there was a scrap of paper about a volunteer exchange scheme with the United States run by Toc H. Jane Richardson had just finished her training and was desperate to get away for a while – but she 'didn't just want to go grape picking'. Her course had encouraged her to feel that she was capable of taking on anything but she knew that she wasn't: 'I realised that I came from an extremely comfortable background and a very loving family . . . I just felt, what in the world do I know about what it's like to be socially deprived?' So, aged 23 and 'quite green', she went to New York to spend the summer working at Fountain House, a rehabilitation centre of a pioneering kind for those who had suffered from a mental illness.

Jane had specifically wanted this placement rather than any of the others – which included working with children or with drug addicts. Her father had been a charge nurse in a psychiatric hospital and she had always picked the psychiatric options at college. She had had a number of acquaintances and friends who had suffered breakdowns and one close associate at university had taken her own life. So, always having known the person before the illness, she 'never thought there was anything odd or different or strange . . . If you've known someone, whatever the subsequent issue it can never outweigh the fact that you've known them as a person, an individual.' But she did think that they were special – their experience held a kind of fascination for her: 'I think, without being sentimental about it, that they plumb the depths of themselves in a way that most of us just never do in our lives.' She could not see this as a negative thing, despite the incredible pain associated with what she interpreted as an intense self-knowledge: 'These friends of mine were often at their most brilliant when they were actually quite unwell . . . at their most alive and creative just before they got out of control.'

Her four months in New York were 'wonderful – I was bowled over'. She felt immediately at home in Fountain House and was entirely comfortable with the way of working there. Her training had led her to see herself as 'the expert' from whom clients would seek advice. But Fountain House was deliberately run with a skeleton staff so that the 350 'members' ran the whole show, doing everything from the cooking and the cleaning to running the coffee bar and the thrift shop. The staff were entirely dependent on them – especially Jane. Fresh from middle-class England, she suddenly found herself living in what turned out to be a particularly rough area of New York:

> Heroin alleys, people openly shooting heroin in the street, people everywhere in bags in the street . . . it was so cosmopolitan, a melting pot . . . I was suddenly exposed to the whole American dream in all its monstrous manifestations. It was all very heady stuff! And the members showed me New York. They were caring for me. It was a relationship of equals.

Fountain House *expected* a lot of people – it made demands on them and the demands were met:

> I just found out so much about the way people *could* function and still actually be, in a clinical sense, totally unwell. Everyone was just treated according to how they were as individual people, rather than purely in terms of their medical life, which is such a primitive way of looking at things. And the staff were not encouraged to feel that they were somehow separate from the people they worked with. And there was this *fantastic* energy in the place – that was the immediate thing that hit you. When I returned to England people said, 'Oh well, it's just the American hype, that's what you can expect'. But I just didn't buy that because these were the very people who were populating our day centres in England and clinging to the walls, completely lacking in motivation.

People will behave, she realised, according to how one expects them to behave.

On her return to England, she was burning to 'spread the word' of the approach to community health care to which she had now been won over. She felt a missionary zeal to tell people that their assumptions were wrong – that there was no need to write anybody off. So, having decided that she could not tolerate working for the social services, she joined the Toc H staff to initiate and coordinate the setting up of 'friendship circles' for the recovering mentally ill in Buckinghamshire. It was not quite what she'd had in mind; an impoverished inner city would have been more like it. But before long she found that she was working harder than she'd ever done in her life before and her confidence and fervour gave way to alarm as she realised what she had taken on and the extent of her isolation and responsibility. Gradually this in turn gave way to a strengthened belief in the philosophy shared by Fountain House and Toc H friendship circles, and to a more genuine confidence as she saw her work begin to bear fruit in a remarkable way.

The first friendship circle had opened in 1975 in Cleveland. It was largely the brainchild of Ann Crouch, then Volunteer Organiser at the North Tees Hospital. Ann was 41 and had been in the post for some 18 months. She was influenced by the increasing emphasis, from the late 1960s, on the importance of self-help groups. It was recognised, for example, that those who had already conquered alcoholism were the people best qualified to help others to conquer it; and serious thought was also being given to the particular contribution that volunteers could make. 'It was to do with enabling people to do things for themselves as much as we could; and about bridging the gap between the inside world and the outside world, which is something a member of the hospital staff can never do.' Ann began to make plans for a day centre for ex-mental patients that would be very different, in its underlying philosophy, to anything on offer anywhere else.

> We weren't going to bring in meals on wheels. The group was going to prepare its own midday meal. People said we wouldn't be able to cook for 20 on an ordinary domestic stove, but with my large family I'd done that many times.

We weren't going to meet on social services or hospital premises, because that smacked of remaining ill. We were going to find a location that was central, in reach of buses, so that people could make their own way in. We weren't going to get the meal subsidised. People should pay for their own food. In hospital the regime is one where things are done to you. We were going to get people doing things in a normal, everyday way.

The group would also be challenging the stigma which every mental patient carries. 'You're never an ex-hysterectomy but you're always an ex-psychiatric patient.' The role of volunteers in the group was not yet immediately clear to Ann, 'but we weren't going to train them to look after poorly people'. Now that thinking *is* clarified and all who attend, whether they've been ill or not, are known simply as members. Toc H had had connections with the North Tees Hospital and Ann got into conversation with one of the members of staff. The day centre she planned wouldn't cost much but it did need a recognised voluntary organisation to sponsor it. Toc H offered and although Ann had some doubts about this idiosyncratic body which seemed to expect her to find both the volunteers and the money herself, she accepted. It was the beginning of a creative partnership which was to influence both sides deeply. The day centre quickly became known as a friendship circle and the network of these circles has now spread into various parts of the country. They are a contemporary expression of the Toc H emphasis on relationships, on personal growth and exploration. They respond to a crying need in a society into which long-term psychiatric patients are being discharged from hospitals that are closing down, often with nowhere to go and no support. But they are not a 'service'; they are a meeting point. In the best circles it is impossible to tell the difference between an 'ex-patient', a member of staff and a volunteer. All members are encouraged to participate equally in the running of the circle: and the first chairman of the first circle was a 'patient'.

Ann's starting point had been a conviction that everybody had their own special gifts and that for each individual there was a time of need and also a time of strength, when he or she was able to give to others. She found that people who had been ill themselves seemed to be especially sensitive to the moods of others. 'They spot your bad days. If I go in not feeling good they'll spot it. Then it's me that's sat down and given a cup of tea.' Some of the most dramatic instances of this can come at unexpected moments and can change people's lives by changing their attitudes to themselves. On one occasion some Toc H volunteers took one of the circles for a walk on a steep and slippery path. One of the volunteers:

> became quite hysterical about the drop at the side. She didn't like heights. Very naturally a man who'd spent many years in hospital walked between her and the drop. He walked beside her for an hour like that, never saying a word. When it was very slippery he took her arm. She was obviously dependent on him at that stage, and that incident led to a change in him. For that hour he'd been the helper. Before, he would come in and stand with his head down until someone told him to take his coat off. If you talked to him he'd answer 'yes', 'no', 'maybe', just one word. Now each week you see him in the kitchen, peeling the spuds and chatting.

Ann believes that this sort of thing happens so often and so powerfully because Toc H took her idea of friendship circles one stage further than she had herself. Her early scepticism gave way to admiration as she watched the way that the staff member she was associated with went about his work:

> without that we'd have slipped into the more usual kind of group – trained volunteers helping poorly people. What I'd seen in him did in fact reflect an aspect of Toc H as a whole and that was what was needed for friendship circles. It was a way of being, rather than just switching on your voluntary hat and switching it off again when you went home. One thing our members had lost in being ill was a way of being. I can't think of another voluntary organisation that could have done the job of circles as admirably as Toc H.

Toc H, in turn, has recognised that circles are going to remain an important focus of the movement as a whole in the 1990s. Recently, there has been an extension of the work in the form of Webb House, a fine building in Middlesbrough which has been developed as a day resource and residential centre for those recovering from a mental illness. It was, again, Ann's brainchild. Her belief in the need for a centre was confirmed when she herself was able to visit Fountain House.

The members of the circles and of Webb speak glowingly of them: 'with the understanding and love they give', as one put it, 'you feel a real person that matters'. Another explains that it was in the friendship circle that he first found people he could really relate to, people who had had similar experiences to him, who accepted him and treated him as a friend. And more than one stresses how much they have learnt about others and how their tolerance has increased through the relationships they have formed.

As for Jane Richardson, it is still the equality, the freedom from having to be an expert, which means most to her, as it had done in Fountain House. She feels free to make mistakes, to have a go and see what happens. The more she works *with* the members (and she has sometimes found it difficult to do this fully), the more she becomes conscious of their common experience – and she believes that this helps her to understand better the *extraordinary* experiences which they have and which she does not share.

Her work and her four years with Toc H have convinced her that the movement as a whole has a message that is of fundamental importance. She is less clear about how it can be put across: 'One of the difficulties is that this kind of message is often only heard in time of crisis, like a war. A war is a great way of making people take stock.' People who have suffered mental illness have in a sense been through a battle all their own: 'One of the reasons circles work is that they catch people in crisis. That's why you can get the "Toc H mix", which we certainly do have in circles.'

Interestingly enough, it is in a residential situation that the ingredients of crisis and of mixture seem to work to best effect. Time and again members refer to the glorious holidays they have enjoyed with the circles in Toc H centres such as Lindridge House in Devon. These have clearly been their high-spots. But it is not just because they provide a chance to get away for those who otherwise would never escape a city or a suburb; it is that they trigger off unusual levels of intimacy and communication. For Jane, the most significant memories are of 'conversations at 2 a.m. with somebody whose life is just totally different from yours; someone who's had a completely different experience of themselves . . . and you have these fantastic conversations . . . There's so much to discuss, so much to talk about . . . such a lot of wisdom.'

16

Surrounded by Laughter

Put Peter East down anywhere in the world and within minutes he would be surrounded by children and he and they would be enjoying a succession of wordless jokes. He seems always to be surrounded by laughter. He's quiet, diffident and extraordinarily humble, yet he has a magnetic quality, a kind of simple innocence combined with shrewd common sense. In 1967, when he was aged 44, he was appointed warden of the Toc H hostel on Tower Hill, in London. A chance meeting led him, with some of the hostel residents, to teach English to young men who had come as teenagers from the Sylhet district of what was then East Pakistan and has, since 1971, been Bangladesh. Despite the grim conditions in which they lived, and their long hours of work in the uncongenial surroundings of clothing sweatshops, Peter found in these young men a friendliness and sense of fun to which his whole being responded.

For 16 years, a period which saw the transformation of frightened newcomers into effective and self-confident community leaders, he worked with young Bangladeshis in the East End of London. And then, at the age of 60, he decided to go to live in Bangladesh, where a remarkable educational and welfare project grew up around him.

The main focus of Peter's work in the East End of London was Number Seven, a hostel where 20 young Bangladeshi men lived together. But it was much more than a hostel. It was a social centre where 100 or more young men would come together every Sunday; it was a resource for the whole community; and it was a place where white community workers were able, in many cases for the first time, to meet Bangladeshis and to become aware of their particular needs. It was open for just nine years but in that time it made an important contribution to the development of the Bangladeshi community, not least through the awareness and self-confidence it gave to its residents, many of whom are now leaders of community organisations in the area.

Linked to Number Seven was a programme of regular weekend camps, arranged with the help of Toc H branches in the London area. As at the hostel, much of the organisation and the practical arrangements were the responsibility of the campers, so that, at one level, Peter East and the other leaders were there as guests. 'If we tried to help with preparing vegetables or anything', says Peter, 'the knife was taken off you immediately – "kindly sit down".'

Peter did not, of course, do all this on his own. His closest colleagues were Caroline Adams and Shah Rahman. Caroline, who was aged 24 when Number Seven opened in 1973, was a youth worker with Avenues Unlimited, a YMCA-sponsored project in the East End. She had worked in refugee camps in Bangladesh during the war of independence and, like Peter, had fallen under the spell of the people. Shah Rahman was a Bangladeshi barrister who devoted much of his spare time to the needs of the Bangladeshi community in the East End. The three used to meet together at least twice a week, usually in a pub. 'That was my support group', says Caroline, 'and I guess the same goes for them as well. We were the three people doing community development work among the Bangladeshi community, all from our different standpoints. You look at the three of us and we're a kind of odd trio. We had a really wonderful relationship, the three of us, and it enabled a whole lot of things to happen. A lot of things came out of those wretched drinking sessions!'

The three of them developed a deep personal friendship. The considerable differences of background and approach did not disrupt the partnership because they were acknowledged and accepted and because all three recognised that the aims which they had in common were much more important than the different beliefs and attitudes which motivated them. The fact that Caroline worked for Avenues Unlimited and Peter for Toc H was to them totally irrelevant. They worked together in mutual trust and confidence, as closely as two colleagues can. Yet, though Caroline and Shah made specific contributions to Number Seven, contributions which only they could make, they both recognise that the project owed its uniqueness and its special flavour above all to Peter East.

In 1973, soon after Number Seven opened, Peter paid his first visit to Bangladesh. He wanted to get to know the families of his East End friends and to learn something of the background from which they came. But his decision to go to Bangladesh was more than a powerful symbol of his genuine interest in the young men with whom he worked, it also subtly changed his relationship with them. Up to that point he had been the teacher and advisor, helping them to adjust to life in London. Now they in their turn were called on to teach and advise him about life in Bangladesh. He needed their help.

The great majority of Bangladeshis in Britain come from the district of Sylhet, in the northeast of the country, and so it was to Sylhet that he went. In the town of Sylhet, and the villages round about, he was an object of intense curiosity. Most people had never seen a white man before. He recalls going to a market and being 'surrounded by, I don't know, between 100 and 200 people, all standing looking at me. Not a smile. Not hostile. Just looking. I was in a chemist's shop one day and so many people surrounded it that the chemist had to close the shop. It was only a shack and the whole thing was rocking. But all you've got to do is just smile and 100 faces light up.'

Gradually he came to the conclusion that he was called to go to live in Bangladesh. It seems right to use the word 'called', though it's probably not a word he would use himself, because his underlying motivation, the thing above all else that makes him tick, is his religious faith. But as a Christian he had been in what many would see as an awkward position; and in Bangladesh that position would be even more awkward. In order to be accepted, and to be able to do the work to which he felt called, he had to overcome the natural suspicion that his real aim was to entice people away from their Muslim faith and convert them to Christianity. Any attempt to spread his own faith would destroy everything he was trying to do. But he never saw himself as an evangelist. He never thought that the spreading of Christianity was his business. His task, as he saw it, was to try, simply and humbly, to live as Jesus would have done. He was there to serve and to love. He sometimes said that his job was not to make the residents of Number Seven Christians but to make them better Muslims. In London and in Bangladesh he didn't try to force anything on people; he tried to awaken the best that was in them.

In April 1983 many of his friends came together in the upstairs room of a pub, to celebrate his sixtieth birthday and to wish him well in Bangladesh. There were residents of Number Seven, young men whom he'd taught to speak English, or taken camping, residents of the Toc H hostel of which he'd been warden, youth workers and community workers, neighbours from the estate where he lived. It was a happy, uproarious and deeply moving occasion. It is doubtful whether anyone else could have brought together such an extraordinary variety of people, such a complete cross-section of East End life.

What everybody wanted to know, of course, was what precisely he intended to do in Bangladesh. What were his plans? And the truth was that he didn't know. He had no detailed plans. He was simply going to live among his friends. By being there, and by having the patience to get to know the real needs and, even more important, the people who would be willing to work with him in meeting those needs, he would learn what there was for him to do.

He stayed initially with the family of one of his London friends, in the village of Burukundi. He spoke no Bengali (he has never learned much of the language) but he had an immediate rapport with the children. 'What tears me apart', he wrote at that time, 'is that most kids have no life, no fun, no games, just suffering; and yet always ready to break through is the child who wants love and laughter.' As they crowded round him he was able to give them some of that love and some of that laughter. And he was able to help a great many individuals. Like the boy, the breadwinner for his family, who was spending three quarters of his meagre wage in getting to work. It was scarcely worth working, except that it gave him self-respect and the hope of something better. Peter bought him a secondhand bicycle and life for that family was transformed. Money which used to be spent on fares could now be spent on food. The health of the younger children showed almost immediate improvement.

Yet he never felt that he could make a long-term contribution in this village. There was no committed local leadership and without that no project could survive beyond the period of his own stay. He'd been in Bangladesh nearly a year when he happened to meet, in a shop in Sylhet town, a man called Harun Ahmed. He felt immediately that here, at last, was someone he could work with. Harun is self-deprecating and mild-mannered but he's the most powerful figure in the village of Khasdobir. Peter sensed at once that Harun cared deeply about the plight of the poor people in his village and was genuinely committed to helping them. He decided to move to Khasdobir.

Khasdobir is a cluster of some 13 villages, though it's impossible for the visitor to tell where one ends and the next begins, and it has a population of about 30,000. It's on the edge of Sylhet town, on either side of the main road which leads to the airport. Apart from this one metalled road there are a maze of earth lanes, which are baked hard by the sun in the dry season but, during the monsoon, turn to slippery mud in which it's almost impossible to keep your footing. There are a few large brick-built houses, all owned by 'londonees' – the term applied to all who work abroad, whether in London or Leicester or Manchester or Kuwait. Most people, however, live in mud-walled huts, built on a framework of bamboo poles, with roofs of thatch or corrugated iron and with blankets hung on a string to form the interior walls. Furniture is just a bed or two, a cupboard and maybe one or two chairs. Some have no furniture at all, living and sleeping on the earth floor.

Harun is, as of right, chairman of more or less everything in Khasdobir, including the committee responsible for the government primary school. Although the government pays the teachers, the local community has to provide the building. The Khasdobir school had space for 700 children (in two shifts, half in the morning and half in the afternoon); and there was a waiting list of 300. Harun and his committee had raised a third of the cost of adding a second storey to the building; would Peter's friends in Toc H be able to find the balance? They did.

Scarcely had work started than the monsoon rains began. 'Harun and I', wrote Peter, 'go every day and get soaked, to show solidarity with the workers. Yesterday I bought them tea. A waiter came from the tea shop, balancing a tray of teas on one hand as only waiters can, holding his umbrella in the other, the rain being torrential. He was wading through swirling water knee deep. What's more he hardly spilt a drop. And of course he was bare-footed, treading on stones and goodness knows what.'

That was written in July. In September it was still raining and the flooding, which had already affected much of the surrounding area, reached Khasdobir.

> In the low lying ground of the village the water was chest-high. Harun and I and my English class of 15 youths, who are now becoming the village action group, decided the elderly, widows and disabled should be helped. There was no boat in the village, and no question of hot food, or food that could be cooked, because cooking is done at floor level on mud stoves that had been washed away. So we got plastic sacks of bread rolls. These we carried on our heads, and formed a chain by holding hands, and waded in the water chest-high delivering them. At times the water was too deep and some of the group would have to swim. We kept this up for five hours. It was for me scaring and fun and tragic, all mixed up. I was scared of water snakes, but had no problem there, had problems with leeches though. The fun bit was that many of the stranded children were laughing, clapping and jumping up and down with delight, both at the rolls and at me trying to keep my balance in the water. Also, not knowing the meaning, politely asking: 'What is your father's name? Stand up. Sit down. Are you fine?' They clearly had no idea of the danger they were in. The tragic side, of course, they had lost everything.

That shared experience created a strong bond between Peter and Harun and the group of young men. Because of his determination to build something that would last Peter moved quite soon to give the group a formal identity. The Khasdobir Youth Action Group was set up officially with, of course, Harun as its chairman.

As the work on the school extension continued the Group concentrated on providing materials to rebuild over 100 flood-damaged houses and on helping, where they could, individuals in desperate need. Like the widow with five children who lived with her brother and his family until, through illness, he was no longer able to support her. The Group built her a small house and provided money to enable her to start work making baskets and mats from bamboo. Or like Muressa Bibi, about whom Peter wrote:

> We think she is about 90 years old, almost blind. She lives alone in a little hovel. She has no furniture, sleeps on the earth floor, her bedding is just rags. She has no income and is very feeble. She cannot go out every day with her begging bowl because of her health. She has no known relations. I have never known her complain. She always jokes, says I'm trying to date her! We have arranged with one of the boys from the school to visit her twice a day, apart from Harun's and my visits. This lovely old lady is so content. Her only problem, she says, is that she can offer us nothing but her prayers.

In the same letter he spoke about his first Christmas in the village of Khasdobir, where he lived in one room at the back of a shop. He had electricity, and piped gas on which to cook, but water had to be fetched from a tube well each day.

> On Christmas Eve [he wrote] the headmaster and some teachers and about 30 children and Harun and the school committee arrived out of the blue, loaded with coloured papers, and made lovely Christmas decorations. They even brought a tree and lights. On Christmas Day we had a children's party here. It was packed. The village produced a huge cake – how it was done is a great mystery to me but we all had a great time. Anyway, we were all able to get away from the reality of life here for a few hours. I think I will always remember those laughing, happy faces, and be grateful for the way this village has accepted me.

The extended school is a strikingly beautiful building, with an elegant outside staircase leading to the new upper floor, and thin white pillars framing the upper and lower verandas. It now has space for 1400 children in two shifts; it also acts as the social centre for the village. By the time it was completed, in the spring of 1985, the Khasdobir Youth Action

Group had already started what was to be its major innovation – Schools under the Sky.

Being on the edge of the town Khasdobir is not an agricultural village. People scrape a living pedalling cycle rickshaws or as labourers employed on a daily basis when work is available. Most of the poorest people are illiterate and therefore unable to teach their children the alphabet, which is a requirement for admission to primary school. The Schools under the Sky, therefore, were set up to ensure that these children get the schooling which their parents never had. Each morning 100 or more children gather together under the trees and are taught by the young members of the Action Group. They squat on the ground, writing on slates, chanting letters and numbers. Most mornings a group of parents stands looking on, shy but at the same time proud, and the teachers are able to get across some basic lessons in hygiene to them.

Though these Schools under the Sky are now part of the life of the village of Khasdobir, a great deal of gentle persuasion was needed to convince people of the value of education. Children, after all, can work, pushing handcarts or collecting firewood for sale in town, and the money they earn is an essential part of the family budget. Peter talks about a boy of eight who is the breadwinner for his widowed mother and his younger sisters. At seven each morning he takes sweets made by his mother and offers them for sale at a roadside market. He does go to school (he's in the afternoon shift) but afterwards he picks up the sweets his mother has made during the day and returns to the market until eight or nine in the evening. That's the pattern of life for a great many children in Bangladesh. Nonetheless there are now six Schools under the Sky, attended by about 800 children in all. Each year some 300 children go forward to primary school, children who, without the Khasdobir Youth Action Group, would have no education at all.

A couple of miles from Khasdobir the apparently endless flatness of Bangladesh is broken by a few low hills and on their gentle slopes are tea gardens. Tea was first planted there a little over 100 years ago and the estate manager still lives in the elegant and spacious bungalow built at that time. The first tea companies were Scottish and there's still a sign pointing to the golf club which they established, though only the clubhouse remains. The workers were Hindus brought from South India. Divided from the indigenous population by language, religion and culture they have remained a separate community. Peter felt sure that a School under the Sky was desperately needed on the tea estate. The members of the Action Group weren't keen and the managers of the tea estate were suspicious. Everyone told him that the workers had no interest in education; only a handful of children attended the one-room school on the estate. Quietly, gently, he persisted. And when the School under the Sky eventually opened 160 children turned up. Now two of the six Schools under the Sky are on tea estates.

Another important piece of work initiated by the Khasdobir Youth Action Group is the clothing workshop where women, widows and their daughters, learn to make clothes. Not only are they learning a skill which will enable them to earn a living; they are also growing in self-confidence. In February 1986 Peter wrote: 'Five young widows have just left my house, they were after clothes for their children . . . It was not till I wrote that down that I realised just how surprising that is. They were not veiled, they didn't hide behind a tree, they smiled, looked directly at me and spoke. They are from our training workshop and already they "walk tall".'

When he left London Peter said he planned to stay in Bangladesh for five years. He returned home on leave in the summer of 1986, quite seriously ill with hepatitis, and that reinforced his conviction that he should leave in April 1988, when he would be 65. Much of his last year was spent convincing people that he really would be leaving, and setting up a formal committee structure to ensure that the work would continue.

Not only has it continued, it has grown. Functional literacy classes for women tea-workers have been started. These women are paid according to how much tea they pick and literacy is therefore important in the simple sense that they need to be able to check how much their basket weighs, and to see that the supervisor has written down the correct figure. But what in the long run will prove more important is that these women, like others with whom the project works, are growing in self-confidence and in their ability to work together to improve their lives.

It was just over four years since Peter East had first met Harun Ahmed in a shop in Sylhet. In that time they had established a project which had brought education for the first time to many hundreds of children, had given widows the chance of earning an independent living and had helped numerous destitute people with the small amounts of money which in Bangladesh make the difference between life and death. But to talk just in terms of classes begun and individuals helped is to miss the uniqueness of this particular project. Every visitor comments on its extraordinary atmosphere, an atmosphere which reflects the personality of Peter himself. Moyra Blake and Mila Caley, both of whom were working with Bangladeshi students in London, visited Khasdobir in the winter of 1984–5. In their report they wrote:

> On first touring the area with Peter and Harun two main factors hit you. One is that many people here are living in destitute or semi-destitute conditions; the other is that something good is going on here. There is an atmosphere of optimism and good humour. People laugh and joke a lot. Perhaps the many children bear the greatest testimony to the positive feeling – everywhere they greet you with golden smiles, shout 'good morning!' or, in their own language, '*kemon acho*!', follow you for a while, or rush to hold hands with Peter.

To walk through the village with Peter as the children call out their greetings, or to enter the school playground and be immediately surrounded by shining eyes and clutching hands, is an unforgettable experience. A London teacher, who visited Bangladesh some months after Peter left, said she could tell at once where he had been by the attitude of the children. Most children stood a little way off, shy, eyes lowered; in Khasdobir the children were self-confident, welcoming and friendly.

And there's something else, less obvious but perhaps even more important. Peter was, in his quiet, undemonstrative way, seeking to change attitudes. Everyone in the village called him simply Peter bhai (brother Peter); and the elite of Sylhet were profoundly shocked when rickshaw drivers shouted out their greetings, calling him Peter bhai as though he were an equal. But it went further than that. Many of the poorest people have come to Khasdobir from other districts to seek a living in Sylhet town. While everyone agreed that the poor of the village must be helped, no one in the Group wanted to help these 'foreigners'. Nor did they want to help the Hindus on the tea estates. Slowly, gently, he challenged such attitudes. About a year after moving to Khasdobir he wrote:

> It's slow but sure. The Eid Festival highlighted this point. We visited 380 of the most destitute families and gave them a food parcel of rice, flour, sugar and powdered milk. Nearly all these families were 'outsiders'. Together we were able to see the appalling conditions fellow human beings have to suffer and of course when one is confronted with such suffering it opens up avenues of thought and talk of why this should be and what can we, the Group, do about such problems. Group members sit around at night, mainly at the school which is undoubtedly the focal point of the village, wrestling with these problems. Can you imagine our schools back home being used as drop-in centres at night? People wander in, pull up a chair, and there's a spontaneous meeting. It often reminds me of a continual Toc H project.

Just before he left Bangladesh a member of the Group said to him: 'You've taught us that there aren't any foreigners.'

He had been in Khasdobir for just over four years. He had established a project which continues to flourish. He had given some of the poorest people a new sense of self-confidence and of their own worth. Above all, he had gone a long way towards changing the ingrained attitudes of a whole village.

17

A Better Hindu

Toc H, says Satish Visavadia, a youth and community worker in his late twenties, made him, for the first time, proud of his Asian culture. It helped him to discover his identity as a black Briton. It made him a better Hindu.

Satish speaks English as though he'd been in England all his life, but his first 11 years were spent in East Africa. His family were tailors, serving the indentured labourers brought from India to build the railways. An initially successful business gradually declined so that when, in 1974, they had either to become Kenyan citizens or to retain their British passports and move to Britain, they felt they had little choice but to go. They settled in Leicester, Satish and his parents and his seven brothers and sisters. They live comfortably now in two adjoining houses but life was hard at first, despite the help of relatives already living in Leicester. 'My mum worked, my father worked, my eldest brother worked – he had no education at all in this country. My school days were spent pretty well in struggle.'

Satish met Toc H through his sister, who is physically handicapped and was then, in 1978, at a special school. He was invited to a disco for pupils from her school, run by a group of young people who called themselves the Impact Group of Toc H. 'There for the first time I saw fellowship between black and white. It was the first time I'd come across a mixed group, male and female. It was really good. One evening with the group had given me so much I thought I'd like to get involved.' The friendships he made in that group have lasted. 'Only two days ago I had a telephone call. She said: "I'm ringing you because I'm really missing you." That fellowship is still there. She's in London now. It's 10 years on but our feelings towards these people are still the same.

They're just as strong. These things will be with us all our lives. They led us to areas of ourselves we didn't know existed.'

It was an experience which lasted a little under four years; but it completely changed the course of his life. It was partly that he'd always felt himself subject to authority, whether at school or at work. There had always been somebody to tell him what to do. 'Suddenly, for the first time, I was able to make decisions that affected my own life. Nobody else controlled it.' And then, as he got more deeply involved with this group of young people, of different races, different religious traditions, different cultures, he found paradoxically that he was getting in touch with his own culture and his own faith. He was going through 'a very rebellious stage', rejecting everything in his own background. It was apparently insignificant things which began a process of change. 'People were saying: "You're a Hindu." And I thought: "Well, am I?" People said, you know, "We love your curries." I always wanted to say: "I hate them, don't mention them." But for the first time I was seeing the positive side of my identity. I haven't looked back since. I have been much stronger in my own faith.'

His faith is stronger because he hasn't meekly accepted beliefs handed down by his elders; he has discovered for himself the things that are important to him. His naturally questioning attitude was encouraged by Toc H but it is not one that makes him popular within the Hindu community. 'You're not supposed to question, they get very upset about it. Even when my mum is talking about the Ramayana, the great Hindu epic – and I believe all that – I say: "This is drama. What is the fact, what really happened?" And she'll say: "Here's the book." And I say: "Well, who wrote the book? How did he know?" And she'll say: "Ah, you're not supposed to say that." '

The Toc H group was important, not just to Satish but to the whole family. All four brothers belonged. 'It was only there that we got together. For the first time we were sitting and talking about things that concerned us. We couldn't do that at home. It was only Toc H that brought us together.'

As he became more aware of his own family and his own culture, however, he also became more aware of the insularity of many in the British Asian community. 'To be honest, in Africa we were more together as an Asian community. In Africa I had Muslim friends, I had Hindu friends, I had Sikh friends, I had African friends. The only Muslims I know here are through Toc H. We don't benefit from the goodness and the richness in other people.' This insularity may in the past have helped to keep the cultural tradition alive and pure, but young people increasingly want to break out and to adapt the tradition to the modern world. 'If we deny them that they'll rebel and go somewhere else. That's what's happening effectively.'

This insularity is, in part at least, a defensive reaction to the experience of white racism, the natural response of a minority group that feels itself oppressed. 'A lot of black people, without meeting individuals, will say: "I hate white people." We were saying to our families, and to our extended family, hang on, not everybody is like that, we've come across some extremely nice people, they've been open and honest.'

Through the Impact Group Satish met a lot of white people but the first meeting was never easy. 'Would they see me as Satish, as a black person, as a "Paki", or as someone who has just come from India and is completely uneducated? People often didn't see me as Satish, they saw me as the "Paki" on the street.' He visited Toc H branches in villages which had never seen a black person; and was surprised by the ignorance of many of those he met. One man even asked him what colour his blood was. But he also found the Toc H members very open. 'They will listen to you if you will listen to them. They were often surprised at the articulate way we were able to express ourselves. We were an example of black people, that we were British, we were brought up in this country, we lived in clean houses like anybody else, we had an upbringing which was very disciplined. All these values they had seen as Christian values and suddenly here was this Hindu who had got the same values. If I heard people saying things I didn't agree with I didn't just sit there. I shouted loudly, said: "I don't agree with you, mate." I made lots of very good friends.'

Some of these Toc H friends he invited to his brother's wedding. 'Some of them had never been to an Asian wedding and for them to see a sort of cultural ceremony was the experience of a lifetime. So there was a bit of an exchange of culture.' People outside Toc H, however, continually expressed surprise at finding that he, a Hindu, belonged to a movement which they had thought was exclusively Christian. 'People think fellowship only comes with Christianity; but fellowship is fellowship whoever you are.'

As well as putting Satish in touch with his own culture, and with the white community, his membership of the Toc H Impact Group led him gradually to the conviction that he should give up his work as an engineer. Toc H offered him a full-time volunteer job in return for board and lodging, as a preparation for a youth and community work course. His parents were unhappy about this change of direction. He was throwing up a recognised profession to take up work that they didn't understand. But Satish himself had no doubts. 'If something moves me I will actually go and do it. I won't pull out. My style is like that.'

His year with Toc H was 'really good'. It included three weeks in Germany, leading a group of volunteers running a play scheme for British army children. 'Taking command of a situation as a black person in an army garrison was quite an experience.' There were a lot of people in the army 'who couldn't take black people, looked down on you all the time'. But it was nonetheless a very positive experience. 'The sheer trust they put in you is enormous. You've got to deliver. That was a real challenge for me and I enjoyed it.'

For much of that year he was in a completely white working environment. 'Just my being there brought up issues which wouldn't otherwise have been issues at all.' After that experience he was understandably angered when one of the colleges to which he applied for training in youth and community work assumed that his future career would be solely within the Asian community. He felt insulted by this under-valuing of his abilities and he is tempted to let them know of his recent appointment to work in a group of Warwickshire villages where his is the only black face.

He is convinced that Toc H can do for many other young people what it has done for him. And he sees an increasing need for Toc H in a society which seems to be more than ever divided. There is 'a strong lobby from various religions to have their own schools, almost their own communities'.

But it's not only ethnic and religious division. He points to the mutual suspicion between neighbouring villages. There's a desperate need for people to get to know each other as individuals, to get behind the stereotypes which reinforce hostility.

In his more pessimistic moments he has a deep concern about the future in what he sees as a society changing for the worse in all kinds of ways. 'There's no security – as a family we've talked about this. We have a background of migration. In the next 20 years we might have to migrate somewhere else. These are issues worrying people like myself.' Some people, successful businessmen for example, respond by shutting themselves in their own little world. 'But we don't just live in a capitalistic society. We live in a society where people do have feelings. There is human bonding. There is care. We also have to think about fellowship and where you're going to get your fellowship and your support, because if you don't you're going to crack up. *We've* done it through Toc H.'

But if Toc H is going to respond to the new challenges and opportunities it must, he believes, market itself much more effectively. There are, after all, a lot of organisations competing for the same volunteers. And it must have a clear and comprehensible policy. 'We're in a climate where those who know what they're about are going to be successful. What's Toc H policy on apartheid, for instance? We don't say, we believe in breaking down barriers and therefore we must work to end apartheid. Toc H is probably doing it, but it needs to *say*, we don't believe in it, we want to break it down.'

The greatest obstacle, for young people like him, is that Toc H is perceived as being only for white Christians. One of his fellow full-time volunteers, now an Anglican priest, 'had the right attitudes and perceptions. The Christian aspect for him was to look for himself, his personal self, where he was in life. People would tell him that it's Christian values and all that, but he insisted that it was about people finding themselves; and that that's a challenge that continues till the day you die. . . And I thought, I'm not stupid, I'm not the only one thinking like that.'

He retains a strong personal commitment to offering others the opportunities through Toc H that he has had. In the autumn of 1988 he took a group of Asian girls from Small

Heath, Birmingham, where he was then working, to the birthplace of Toc H in Poperinge, Belgium. There was a great deal of apprehension in the group beforehand, partly because none of the girls had been abroad before, and partly because, as they looked at slides of war cemeteries and of Talbot House, it seemed to them as though they were going to spend the week living in a church. Everything they saw in advance spoke to them of Christianity. 'When we were actually there what we experienced was completely different. The girls changed their view from day one.' They visited museums and saw photographs which brought home to them the horror of war. They found the grave of a 14-year-old soldier – 'That really hit hard.' They visited the Menin Gate in Ieper, where the names of 55,000 men with no known grave are recorded, column after column after column of neatly carved names; and among them were Asian names. 'The girls were shocked. Suddenly they would see Gupta – that's my name, how did that get there?' Words like 'conflict' and 'reconciliation' suddenly became urgent realities.

The girls, like Satish himself a few years earlier, became more aware of their own culture. 'Two of the girls had completely rejected their Asian origin. For the first time they were proud to be Asian.' They performed a dance one evening, to demonstrate something of their cultural heritage to the people of Poperinge. 'They turned up in masses, the whole house was buzzing. It was great.' One of the girls said afterwards: 'For the first time I was proud to be what I am.' Later one of the parents said: 'My girl has completely changed.' And all this in less than a week. 'It was such a powerful time.' For some of the girls the chapel, despite its Christian furnishings, became a place where they could withdraw, where they could reflect quietly on all they had seen and done, and what it meant to them. As they did so they were at one, despite the gulf of years and the differences of cultural and religious tradition, with those who first used that Upper Room.

18

The Way of Friendship

A few years ago, in his sixties, Tom Gulliver visited China. He was one of a number of delegates from all over the world representing the main religions at an inter-faith conference. Curious and conscious of his opportunity, he decided to spend two weeks afterwards travelling around by train. He found it fascinating and was delighted by everyone's friendliness. There was one especially significant evening – in Xian, the only city where he hadn't arranged for an official guide. He met a Chinese businessman in the hotel who asked if he could join him. 'We ate a meal together and we spent the evening going round, visiting the pagodas and the great mosque. It was marvellous – oh, to be touring this city with this Chinese man I'd only just met, talking religion all the time.'

He spends most of his time 'talking religion'. He worked for many years as a civil servant and then joined the Toc H staff, partly in order to develop inter-faith dialogue. Then, in his early retirement, he put his energy into his work as the Honorary General Secretary of the World Congress of Faiths, an organisation founded in 1936 to promote dialogue among the world's religions. For several years he travelled up to London every week, a three-hour journey from his seaside bungalow. He worked in the WCF office near Notting Hill for two or three days and stayed overnight at the Quaker Penn Club near Euston. At home the work continued – he read, telephoned and did paper work on behalf of the Congress. He attended and arranged lectures, meetings and conferences. In 1988, he brought over from Tübingen the leading Catholic theologian Hans Küng for a strenuous weekend of dialogue with representatives from Islam, Hinduism and Buddhism. By the end of the conference, Tom was exhausted but elated. He'd spent the days listening to the public debates;

the evenings continuing them over dinner with Küng and the other speakers. And over lunch or tea he would be off, at the least prompting, on an energetic discourse on revelation, reincarnation or resurrection. His excitement is not expressed in flamboyant gesture or rapid delivery. Still and self-contained, he expounds his theories and releases his anger or enthusiasm in a slow and grainy voice deliberate in emphasis, distinctive in the mild Welsh of its cadence.

His early religious experience was more conventional. Brought up in Newport during the Depression, he was a regular attender at the Church in Wales, encouraged but not accompanied by his mother. His father, who died when Tom was five, had been a born-again Christian; but her own faith was in socialism. The house was full of party members and alive with political discussion – he remembers the arguments between supporters of the Marxist and 'moderate' wings of the party. He's remained a life-long supporter of the Labour Party and was once very active in it. But 'I did become disillusioned, because it doesn't matter what organisation – whether it's a political party, Toc H, the YWCA or whatever – when you get inside there are always personality clashes. You wonder why some people are in it. What one has to *try* to do is to keep people in it that one wishes were not . . . it's that tension which is so creative; it's a kind of dialectic out of which something new comes.'

It was from his mother – not from any Church – that he learnt 'the Social Gospel'. Despite their great poverty, she was always ready to share the food when beggars came to the door. His father's influence on him was more elusive, for Tom remembers him only 'vaguely and traumatically'. 'I was with him when he died. He collapsed in the street. One moment he was there, the next he wasn't. I was standing in a doorway with no one.' As a child he wasn't given the opportunity to grieve and there was no question, in his environment, of analysing or expressing emotions. It wasn't until he was in his middle years that he realised not only that he had not mourned but that he was burdened by guilt. He had obscurely believed, as a child, that he had caused his father's death. Psychology, rather than religion, enabled him to resolve this tension – although he does not think the two can be so easily distinguished. A psychologist such as Jung is essentially religious and his first reading of him was 'like a conversion. I wanted to tell everyone "Have you read Jung? You really ought to. I mean it'll transform your life, you'll be a different person . . ." Just like "Have you found Christ? Are you saved?" I found all my own feelings related in his books and I began to understand what was happening.'

One of the things he discovered was that he'd been spending his life looking for a father figure, an 'older man to whom I could relate as a guide, counsellor or whatever. Later, I came to realise what a nuisance I must have been!' Several such figures feature when he describes his involvement with Toc H, which he first came across when working in Darlington in 1955. He went along to a meeting of the local branch because he'd heard that it was involved in a great variety of voluntary work, and since he wasn't quite sure what it was he wanted to do, this was attractive. He was appalled by the amateurishness of his first meeting; by the next he was 'hooked'. What impressed him was the atmosphere, the 'acceptance' and above all the fact that 'there was no conflict between the claims of Toc H and its practice at that branch. That was what was so meaningful. It was different from a political party, it was different from the Church – because it was one, it was a whole experience.'

It was Toc H that brought him back into the Church. He had moved away in his twenties because he felt that the Establishment and the Church should be quite distinct, and that it was the duty of Christian leaders to speak out against the Second World War. They should be making it clear that violence and patriotism were not the teachings of the Gospels. Not that he had any doubts that the war was a just war and he was clear that it was his personal duty to volunteer in order to fight Hitler's 'evil regime'. He never adopted his mother's fierce pacifism, even when he became a Quaker in later life. And his rejection of the institution of the Church was not a denial of God: 'I don't know what that symbol G-O-D means but I've never had any doubts about that *reality*, even as a child.' As he became involved in Toc H at regional and then national level, he thought more and more about the ethos of the movement. One man, 'my guru in Toc H, showed me how it brought together my two interests of politics and the Church. A religious basis to the changes you want to make in society – that to me is what Toc H has always been about.' He'd gone to do a job of work; he stayed because of a spiritual discovery.

He regards the 'Four Points' of Toc H as 'a work of genius' and the fourth one, which speaks of the 'Kingdom of God' as containing the essence of the movement's message. 'I don't see the Kingdom in evangelical terms of "Are you saved, brother?" I see it in terms of equality, of helping people, of one of the sayings of the early Quakers of "helping one another up with a tender hand". Whatever we have, we have to share – and this is something I inherited from my mother. And this is what Toc H was all about.' He was impressed by the fact that there was no subscription: 'You simply gave what Toc H meant to you.' It was a lay movement which was untrue to itself whenever it gave the staff too much power and 'saw them as a kind of priesthood . . . I've always had hang-ups about priesthoods!' or when it became preoccupied in a desperate search for a leader to replace its charismatic founder. For him Toc H, like Christianity itself, is about *community*: 'It demonstrates that it is possible for people of different education and different aspirations and different work to be friends, and the basis of that friendship is equality.'

For a number of years, Toc H (and the branches in Darlington and St Albans in particular) dominated his life. He also found, through the influence of Toc H, that he became very involved in the work of ecumenism. Then he was introduced to the World Congress of Faiths by a staff padre 'at a time when I was ready for it'. It began to seem to him that dialogue between religions was rapidly replacing dialogue between denominations as the most urgent and exciting spiritual task of the day.

It was a Buddhist abbot, the Venerable Ajahan Sumedho, who had the most profound impact on Tom at this stage. He met him at a WCF weekend on the subject of suffering and listened to him 'talk about it as something that is not real and that you can almost dismiss. I got furious with him at this nonsense and I can remember him laughing!' Later, they became friends, and Tom came to see what he was getting at: 'It's not that you don't suffer but you don't hang onto it – and I think we do, you see . . . You should just accept that this is what is happening to you. And this was an eye-opener for me. It tied up with what I'd just started reading in Jung. Jung believes that neurosis is a good thing because it's indicating that there's something you must do, there's something you must change about your situation in one way or another.'

When he worked on the development of inter-faith for Toc H in the 1970s, the response was disappointing. So few people turned up to some of the weekends he organised that he felt embarrassed at having brought his speakers along under false pretences. It was one of many factors that led to his disillusionment with Toc H – or at least to a recognition that he had moved on to a different way of 'building the Kingdom'. Inter-faith was a fulfilment rather than a denial of his Christianity and he was frustrated by the voices raised in protest at the 'threat' to Toc H's Christian identity. On the contrary, he points out that his work was concerned with dialogue, not conversion. He himself has never been tempted to switch even to one of the Eastern religions to which he is particularly drawn and has never even had to question whether or not he was a Christian: 'I always ask myself – is this thing in another teaching that appeals to me, is it consistent with the Gospels – with what *Jesus* said, not with what the Church said? And I've never found an inconsistency.'

Feeling he could not justify his salary he left the staff to work for WCF, where he felt he could be of more use. But even so, he feels that it is only now that the work of inter-faith is really spreading out beyond a small circle of enthusiasts. After high immigration rates in the 1950s and 1960s, Britain has become a multicultural society. Christian schoolchildren mix with those from other religious backgrounds and are far more open than their parents as a result. The 'relevance' of dialogue is now evident. Inter-faith is not an academic process: it is only by *meeting* people of other faiths that their beliefs can have any real impact.

This is how his own interest began. In 1942 he went out to India with the army and for the first time met people of a different faith to his own. 'I realised that for most people religion isn't a matter of conversion. Conversion may come later, into a deeper understanding or whatever. But usually it's the family you're born into, that's all.' Unlike some of his fellow soldiers, he did not feel superior to the Indians he came across: they were not 'wogs' to him but individuals. 'The bearer who brought me a cup of tea in the mornings and cleaned up the place – I looked on him as a friend, as a person I knew, and not simply as a person to be ordered about.' He admits – in language which shows how far he stretches the norms of Christian theology – that he did have a special affinity for India: 'I suspect I was there in a previous incarnation, because I feel a great empathy.' But the roots of his attitude lay in his socialism as much as in religion: 'I was there at the time of the Gandhi riots and, being a political person, I sympathised with what they were doing.' One day in Ranchi, he found himself walking up through the bazaar towards three Indians coming from the opposite direction, arm in arm 'and obviously looking for trouble'. He stepped off the pavement into the road to let them pass: 'Others would have seen it as an insult to the flag or something stupid. But I sympathised, I knew, and I understand the outbreak of violence in black areas in this country. Because I'm at my most angry when I am at my most powerless. And I too grew up in an area of deprivation.'

He differed also from his fellows in taking the trouble to read the *Bhagavad Gita*. He has no idea why he read it nor why it made such a profound impression on him. But he does remember being struck by two things – the similarities between Krishna and Christ and the 'common sense' of the teaching. The idea that you must strive to do *well* whatever you are called to do appealed to his instinct that acceptance (of a dynamic variety) rather than struggle was the key to life. The emphasis on individual religious experience, on *living* the faith, also appealed to someone with such a powerful mistrust of the Church. 'The difficulty is that we are expected to accept other people's experience as it is written down and to accept Scripture, whereas the only thing that makes sense is one's own experience.'

He was to find this same emphasis, this same reluctance to impose a creed, in the Quakers. This was much later in life, when he was living in Portishead in the 1970s and working for Toc H. Silence and simplicity, further characteristics of Quaker spirituality, had been increasingly important to him. But it was an Anglican communion service which made him realise how far he had moved. Communion had always been of deep personal significance to him ever since he was a child, although he's at a loss to explain why. But on this occasion:

> I went to communion and afterwards I turned to the person next to me in the pew and they just looked straight past me and never spoke to me; they spoke to the people they knew. And *no one* spoke to me. I looked round for someone to speak to and no one, no one spoke to me. And I thought: 'This is not communion; in *no* sense is it communion. And I stopped going and went to the Quakers.' It was very simple, the point of change. Like a row between people – it comes up about something simple, but it's been building up for a long time.

With the Quakers he has found not only peace but the equality, the lack of a priesthood and of status that are for him essential aspects of a Christian community. But, true to type, he has every respect for other Christian denominations. The Roman Catholics are the most active and forward thinking, he claims, in inter-faith dialogue. Yet in Christianity now as a whole, and indeed in all the religions, he sees something stirring – a new openness to each other's wisdom: 'I don't know what the future is. I feel we're just on the verge, but it could take another 50, 70, 100 years.'

Meanwhile, it's the individual contacts and influences which matter above all for people like Tom Gulliver. On his journey out to China in 1986, he was reading a volume of talks by the Venerable Sumedho, the Buddhist monk who had made such a personal impact on him. 'An Indian lady came up to me in the airport lounge and started talking to me about all the difficulties in her spiritual life. Her husband had been brought up in the Ramakrishna school and it didn't appeal to her. I gave the book to her and I wrote in it. And all the way from Islamabad to Beijing, I could see her in the plane, devouring this book.' It's no coincidence that when he compiled a much-used anthology of Toc H writings some 10 years ago, he called it *The Way of Friendship*.

19

Looking Forward

The world of the 1920s seems utterly remote, a world without travel or television, a world without deep freezes or supermarkets, a world where a few square, black, draughty cars stuttered along on empty roads. State care for the needy was as unimaginable as the computer. Hindus and Buddhists were seen only in the pages of books illustrating the subject peoples of the British Empire.

It's not surprising, then, that the Toc H of the 1920s seems equally remote. It's not just a matter of style, the heartiness and the passion for nicknames; the burning concerns, the things they were trying to achieve, were quite different also. They offered a place where Christians of different denominations could meet each other, could begin to overcome the ignorance, suspicion and fear that kept them apart. The ecumenical movement still has much to do but there are many more opportunities now for people of different denominations to come together. They offered people a way of giving voluntary service, an outlet for idealism, that was not generally available through the Churches or other voluntary organisations. The need for voluntary service is as great as it ever was but Toc H is no longer the sole local avenue for it. It is one of dozens of voluntary groups, all competing for sufficient volunteers to maintain their separate existence.

In the 1920s Britain was still the centre of an empire and Toc H spread quite naturally to all the parts of the map that were coloured red. But it was part of the British presence and as that withdrew only a small remnant was left to seek a new role in a new country. In South Africa that role is obvious and it has done much, quietly and undemonstratively, to bring people together in a climate which has actively discouraged such mixing. Both Peter Ranken and Liz Jones, when they were in South Africa in 1986, helped to build a rural health centre in the beautiful, and evocatively named, Valley of a Thousand Hills. They were '15 kilometres up this dirt road, with no electricity and no fresh water supply'. Yet they were less than an hour's drive from the wealthy modern city of Durban – 'it was a stunning contrast'. Six volunteers from Britain worked alongside local people, volunteers from the huge black township of Soweto and white volunteers from Durban. 'It was a rich experience.'

Britain is now, painfully and with varying degrees of reluctance, rediscovering its European identity at a time when the frontiers of Europe are being pushed ever further east. It will perhaps be in Europe, therefore, rather than in what was once the British Empire, that the future expansion of Toc H will take place. Meanwhile there are other changes, less global in scale, which have a more immediate impact. In the 1920s people expected to join an organisation for life, just as they expected to have one job for life. In today's much more mobile society neither assumption holds good. Many of those we have talked to, though deeply conscious of what they owe to Toc H, have moved on. That will surely lead Toc H radically to re-think its structure and its approach. As at Lindridge House the emphasis increasingly is likely to be on short, one-off, no-strings-attached opportunities.

The members of an organisation, of course, can never view change with the objectivity and dispassionate aloofness of the historian. Some, clinging desperately to what has meant much to them, feel that changes are taking place destructively fast; others are frustrated because changes that are, to them, urgent and essential come about with agonising slowness. But what is ultimately significant about Toc H is not what it has done, or the changing ways in which it has done it; it is the profound impact which, despite all its failings as an organisation, it has had on so many individuals. Time and again people talk about their lives being transformed, about how different they would have been if they had not met Toc H. 'The real things would have passed me by', says Don Lockhart, who joined in 1929. And Liz Jones, who met Toc H 50 years later, says it 'meant an immense amount. I was challenged to think about my priorities in life, the things that mattered to me.'

And, amid all the changes, one thing has remained constant, the attempt to interpret the original experience of Talbot House, Poperinge, in contemporary terms. Time and again people have gone back to that experience and found that it's still fresh, it still has something to say. Any attempt to suggest the future significance of the movement has to start by looking again at what happened 75 years ago in that old white house in Poperinge.

We begin at the large, double doors, each with glazing covered by an intricate, wrought iron screen, and see above them the signboard proclaiming this to be 'everyman's club'. As we go in we find ourselves mixing with all kinds of people, talking, for the very first time, with people quite different from ourselves. In this house all are welcome, whatever their status or background, whatever their education or lack of it, whatever their religious beliefs or lack of them. We are encouraged to break out of the narrow confines in which our lives have been lived, and to meet people whom we have previously despised, been frightened of, stood in awe of.

Those who had had that experience returned home to a society in which managers and workers never talked to each other as fellow human beings, in which professional men and labourers lived completely different lives, in which those who went to public schools were fenced off from the majority of the population. They set about creating small groups in which people could come to recognise their common humanity and overcome their fear of the unknown. Some of them went a stage further. It was all very well to talk about ending class hatred but that could only happen through the removal of the injustices which kept people apart, which meant that some people were so poor they had to send their children to school without shoes, which meant that society had no use for many of those who had fought for it, which meant that your income determined the quality of the health care you received. But the determination to create a better world was not a matter of abstract political theories, it was a response to individuals who had become their friends.

In the Britain of the 1990s we live in a society even more deeply divided than theirs, a society from which many feel alienated or excluded. Beggars are once again a common sight on the streets of London. Growing numbers of people sleep rough on the streets of our cities. Those with AIDS are as excluded from society as medieval lepers. Drugs have created a separate sub-culture. As people expect to live longer they seek the assurance that life can still be fulfilling in old age, that it doesn't end when you retire from full-time work. There is a greater need than ever for an organisation which will help us to find ways of breaking out of our own individual ghettoes and will create a sense of belonging.

At this point it's important to penetrate a little further into Talbot House. Leave the people mingling over cups of tea on the ground floor, go up the steep and narrow stairs and, in the words of one of the notices you passed, 'risk meeting the chaplain'. Over the door of the chaplain's room you see a wooden signboard on which is painted: 'All rank abandon, ye who enter here.' Later, some imagined that this exhortation applied to Talbot House as a whole, but it didn't; and the fact that it didn't was significant. While it's important to recognise that at the level of our deepest needs and deepest joys we share a common humanity, it's also important to recognise that each one of us is different. We're a part of the whole, yet we're unique. In the chaplain's room men were invited to lay aside all their differences and recognise that they were simply fallible human beings. In the rest of the house they were encouraged to acknowledge the different qualities and abilities possessed by each individual and to see them as gifts to be shared, not barriers to keep people apart.

That insight is important in the context of multi-cultural Britain. It's all too easy to say to ourselves: 'They're newcomers' (though we're probably talking about people who were born here) 'and so it's up to them to become like us, to fit in.' But the experience of Talbot House was not the creation of a homogeneous lump but the celebration of the richness of diversity. When Satish Visavadiá took a group of Asian girls to Belgium they said that, for the first time in their lives, they were proud to be Asian. But first they had to be willing to go to Belgium and meet Belgian people. In 1989 there was a project with an unusually varied group of volunteers, including two 16-year-old Asian girls. The person who received the applications immediately phoned the mothers of these two girls in order to assure them, as a mother herself, that their daughters would be safe, would be properly cared for and looked after. Without sensitivity of that kind we will never even get to the point of meeting.

The experience of Talbot House, and the experience of Toc H over the intervening years, is that it *is* possible for people to get to know one another, for unlikely friendships to develop. It happens best in a small group which shares a demanding common task. When the Central Council of Toc H met in November 1989 to set the movement's direction for the new decade it re-affirmed that its fundamental job was to enable 'people to meet who would not otherwise do so'.

That is a challenge to everything that keeps people apart, to every form of racism, explicit or implicit, conscious or unconscious, and to everything which tends to dehumanise people. And it's a theological challenge, too. If you believe in any form of creator God you have also to believe that the differences of character, of ability, of culture – and of religion – are within the purposes of God.

Which takes us back to Talbot House in Poperinge. Another, steeper staircase leads to the loft where hops were once stored, and which is now a chapel. It's a quiet place, far removed from the noise and busyness of the street outside, a place with an atmosphere of peace, intangible, indefinable, yet unmistakable, a place where, like the Little Gidding of which T. S. Eliot wrote, 'prayer has been valid'. When people looked back to what they'd experienced in Talbot House they looked back, not only to the friendships which they'd made downstairs, but also to what they had sensed in that Upper Room.

Talbot House offered everyone a welcome but it also offered a challenge. The chapel posed questions about what it was worth living for and worth dying for, what life was all about. It suggested that the great abstract words, like love and friendship, are as real as the things which you can feel and touch. Many found that the special religious words, words like forgiveness, began to mean something for the first time. They became real in their own experience of life.

And so the Toc H that they created after the war offered both a welcome and a challenge. All were welcome without conditions, yet all were challenged to think about the deepest things of life. Maintaining the balance between the two isn't easy. It's very easy to so emphasise the challenge, by stressing the movement's Christian basis, that only those who have a religious faith will feel welcome, or to so emphasise the welcome, to be so anxious to be open to everybody, that there's no challenge at all. And the way in which the balance is maintained can never be static. In the 1920s the challenge could be expressed in traditional Christian language. It was, quite explicitly, a challenge to examine the claims of Christianity.

Things are very different today. All the great religious traditions have a significant place in British society and interfaith dialogue, as Tom Gulliver has recognised, is an urgent and pressing necessity. For the great majority of the population, moreover, the traditional religious language, particularly the Christian language, has gone dead. It no longer means anything at all. Yet people want to find their own way of expressing their deepest convictions, and they want those convictions to be taken seriously. A young volunteer on a Toc H project who says that the atmosphere of acceptance, of love, of laughter, 'feels so right', is making a profound statement about how life ought to be.

'As much as Toc H has influenced me, I've influenced Toc H as well', says Ann Crouch. 'The picture that Toc H presented was very, very Christian. Prayers all the time, and Anglican prayers at that. One of the first Toc H services I went to was a communion service. Half the members couldn't, or wouldn't, take communion. I sat at the back and thought, how divisive.' Now the talk is about devotions, about quiet time, about reflection. 'I'm sure I've influenced some of that. I'm not sure where it's left Toc H.'

Maybe it has left Toc H on the brink of discovering a new role as an organisation devoted to religious exploration; a place where people, whatever their faith or lack of it, can share with each other their own particular insights and can learn from each other; a place where people can find the sacred in ordinary, everyday things, above all in their relationships with one another. 'It's to do with showing people that there is a different way of living, a different way of thinking about things. It doesn't necessarily have anything to do with God or the Church but it's still very real and tangible.'

The Central Council of 1989, in setting the movement's

direction for the coming decade, adopted a statement reaffirming its religious position in contemporary terms. 'Toc H', says the statement, 'is a journey of discovery.' That journey is both 'the development of loving relationships in every sphere of life' and 'a discovery of meaning, a test of belief, and an exploration of spirituality with an openness to the Christian way'.*

Toc H has, in quite different ways, been a journey for all those to whom we have spoken. For some the journey has been a lifelong commitment to Toc H; for others Toc H has been a signpost, pointing them to other spheres of activity; but for all it has been an exploration into themselves. It may well be that today spiritual renewal is more important than a revival of traditional religious forms. Sue Cumming has been helped to recognise her vocation to the ordained ministry but it is equally significant that Satish Visavadia has been helped to become a better Hindu. For all of them, whatever they believe or find it impossible to believe, the journey has brought to life that part of them which can be called spiritual or religious. It has begun to make sense of the world of intuition and feeling. It has helped them to explore the deep meaning to be found in their own experience, the ordinary, apparently mundane events as much as the things which evoke a sense of awe and wonder. Some begin to find traditional Christian images helpful; others struggle to find a language to talk about their experience. But all of them have become, as Peter Ranken put it, aware of what's happening to them, all of them have, in different ways, responded to the challenge posed by the chapel of Talbot House.

As we leave that Upper Room and go back down the steep stairs the sound of laughter rises to meet us. The images which linger in the mind are the yellow daffodil at the mock funeral recalled by Sue Cumming, and Peter East pulling faces, surrounded by a crowd of laughing children. Sustaining all the serious talk of love and sacrifice and spiritual exploration is a lightness of touch, without which none of it would be possible. 'We played together', said Sue Cumming. 'It brought the child out of us all.' That, too, is part of the legacy of Talbot House in Poperinge.

*For the complete text, see Appendix (pp. 132–3).

Appendix

The full text of the documents which set out the aims of Toc H is as follows:

The Main Resolution
(adopted in 1922)

Remembering with gratitude how God used the Old House to bring home to multitudes of men that behind the ebb and flow of things temporal stand the eternal realities, and to send them forth strengthened to fight at all costs for the setting up of his Kingdom upon Earth; we pledge ourselves to strive:

To listen now and always for the voice of God;

To know his Will revealed in Christ and to do it fearlessly reckoning nothing of the world's opinion or its successes for ourselves or this our family; and towards this end:

To think fairly, to love widely, to witness humbly, to build bravely.

The Four Points of the Compass
(as revised in 1967)

I Friendship: 'To Love Widely'

To provide members with opportunities to develop a spirit of understanding and reconciliation.

Members are called on –

to welcome all in friendship,
to lessen by habit of thought, word and deed the prejudices which divide men,
to see the needs of others as their own.

II Service: 'To Build Bravely'

To enable members, with their varying gifts, to serve their fellows.

Members are called on –
to give personal service,
to study local, national and international conditions and their effect on others, and by their example to challenge their neighbours to seek the way of Christ.

III Fairmindedness: 'To Think Fairly'

To bring to members the knowledge and experience of others.

Members are called on –
to listen always to the views of others,
to find their own convictions,
to influence public opinion so that conflict may be lessened by sympathetic and intelligent understanding.

IV The Kingdom of God: 'To Witness Humbly'

Members are called on –
to acknowledge the spiritual nature of man,
to practise the Christian way of life,
to help the truth to prevail.

The Statement of Re-affirmation
(adopted in 1989)

Toc H is a journey of discovery, a journey which leads both outwards and inwards. What we believe affects how we live, and our experience affects what we believe. There are not two journeys but one, because they depend on each other. As we journey outwards, trying to build a loving society, we also journey inwards, seeking personal wholeness.

The journey outwards is the development of loving relationships in every sphere of life. It is a practical testing out of the principles expressed in the life of Jesus.

The journey inwards is a discovery of meaning, a test of belief, and an exploration of spirituality with an openness to the Christian way.

Our commitment to these simultaneous journeys is based on two principles:

(1) Toc H is open to all. This means that some members are committed to a Church while some are exploring meaning and purpose in life with no allegiance to any Church. There is no credal test for membership.
(2) Toc H is based on Christian insights and has Christian roots. We undertake to test in our own lives the validity of the claims made by Jesus in his teachings and in the way he lived.

We have adopted Light as the symbol of this journey of discovery.